1st EDITION

Perspectives on Modern World History

Watergate

1st EDITION

Perspectives on Modern World History

Watergate

Alexander Cruden

Editor

GREENHAVEN PRESS
A part of Gale, Cengage Learning

GALE
CENGAGE Learning·

Detroit • New York • San Francisco • New Haven, Conn • Waterville, Maine • London

Elizabeth Des Chenes, *Managing Editor*

© 2012 Greenhaven Press, a part of Gale, Cengage Learning.

Gale and Greenhaven Press are registered trademarks used herein under license.

For more information, contact:
Greenhaven Press
27500 Drake Rd.
Farmington Hills, MI 48331-3535
Or you can visit our Internet site at gale.cengage.com.

For product information and technology assistance, contact us at
Gale Customer Support, 1-800-877-4253.

For permission to use material from this text or product, submit all requests online at
www.cengage.com/permissions.

Further permissions questions can be e-mailed to permissionrequest@cengage.com.

Articles in Greenhaven Press anthologies are often edited for length to meet page requirements. In addition, original titles of these works are changed to clearly present the main thesis and to explicitly indicate the author's opinion. Every effort is made to ensure that Greenhaven Press accurately reflects the original intent of the authors. Every effort has been made to trace the owners of copyrighted material.

Cover images © Bettmann/Corbis. Reproduced by permission.

LIBRARY OF CONGRESS CATALOGING-IN-PUBLICATION DATA

Watergate / Alexander Cruden, book editor.
   p. cm. -- (Perspectives on modern world history)
   Includes bibliographical references and index.
   ISBN 978-0-7377-5797-2 (hardcover)
 1. Watergate Affair, 1972–1974. 2. Watergate Affair, 1972–1974--Sources. I. Cruden, Alex.
E860.W335 2012
973.924--dc23   2011048761

Printed in the United States of America
2 3 4 5 6 7 16 15 14 13 12

CONTENTS

The press is the enemy, Richard Nixon often said, and when two young Washington reporters kept digging up connections between the White House and obstruction of justice regarding the Watergate situation, Nixon says a counterattack is justified.

attorney and professor. In a democratic system, the people and their legislators need full access to the facts and findings in order to choose the wisest course of action.

A public policy scholar asserts that the president indeed has the right to keep deliberations secret. The US Constitution gives the executive branch broad powers, including executive privilege. The separation of powers doctrine, when properly applied, prevents abuse of this privilege.

A reporter asserts that the main Watergate source for the *Washington Post,* the man whose identity was concealed as "Deep Throat," was not at all a hero. He argues that the source could have stopped Watergate, but instead chose to leak information for ulterior motives.

Anonymously provided information may sometimes lead news organizations astray, a journalist asserts, but relying on unnamed sources is an essential tool for the good of the country, according to a range of media experts. Watergate's "Deep Throat" is a prime example.

controversy and goes on to make the only confession of guilt he ever made.

experience did not leave him bitter, but
instead humbled, as well as saddened that he
let his country down. Yet he never gave up,
she says.

FOREWORD

"History cannot give us a program for the future, but it can give us a fuller understanding of ourselves, and of our common humanity, so that we can better face the future."

—Robert Penn Warren,
American poet and novelist

The history of each nation is punctuated by momentous events that represent turning points for that nation, with an impact felt far beyond its borders. These events—displaying the full range of human capabilities, from violence, greed, and ignorance to heroism, courage, and strength—are nearly always complicated and multifaceted. Any student of history faces the challenge of grasping the many strands that constitute such world-changing events as wars, social movements, and environmental disasters. But understanding these significant historic events can be enhanced by exposure to a variety of perspectives, whether of people involved intimately or of ones observing from a distance of miles or years. Understanding can also be increased by learning about the controversies surrounding such events and exploring hot-button issues from multiple angles. Finally, true understanding of important historic events involves knowledge of the events' human impact—of the ways such events affected people in their everyday lives—all over the world.

Perspectives on Modern World History examines global historic events from the twentieth-century onward by presenting analysis and observation from numerous vantage points. Each volume offers high school, early college level, and general interest readers a thematically

1

arranged anthology of previously published materials that address a major historical event, with an emphasis on international coverage. Each volume opens with background information on the event, then presents the controversies surrounding that event, and concludes with first-person narratives from people who lived through the event or were affected by it. By providing primary sources from the time of the event, as well as relevant commentary surrounding the event, this series can be used to inform debate, help develop critical thinking skills, increase global awareness, and enhance an understanding of international perspectives on history.

Material in each volume is selected from a diverse range of sources, including journals, magazines, newspapers, nonfiction books, personal narratives, speeches, congressional testimony, government documents, pamphlets, organization newsletters, and position papers. Articles taken from these sources are carefully edited and introduced to provide context and background. Each volume of Perspectives on Modern World History includes an array of views on events of global significance. Much of the material comes from international sources and from US sources that provide extensive international coverage.

Each volume in the Perspectives on Modern World History series also includes:

- A full-color **world map**, offering context and geographic perspective.
- An annotated **table of contents** that provides a brief summary of each essay in the volume.
- An **introduction** specific to the volume topic.
- For each viewpoint, a brief **introduction** that has notes about the author and source of the viewpoint, and that provides a summary of its main points.
- Full-color **charts**, **graphs**, **maps**, and other visual representations.

- Informational **sidebars** that explore the lives of key individuals, give background on historical events, or explain scientific or technical concepts.
- A **glossary** that defines key terms, as needed.
- A **chronology** of important dates preceding, during, and immediately following the event.
- A **bibliography** of additional books, periodicals, and websites for further research.
- A comprehensive **subject index** that offers access to people, places, and events cited in the text.

Perspectives on Modern World History is designed for a broad spectrum of readers who want to learn more about not only history but also current events, political science, government, international relations, and sociology—students doing research for class assignments or debates, teachers and faculty seeking to supplement course materials, and others wanting to improve their understanding of history. Each volume of Perspectives on Modern World History is designed to illuminate a complicated event, to spark debate, and to show the human perspective behind the world's most significant happenings of recent decades.

INTRODUCTION

Watergate is a story of flawed heroes and interesting villains. They came together by plan, by circumstance, and by chance to create one of the major episodes in American history, culminating with the only resignation ever of a US president. Numerous players took turns in the spotlight and shadows.

As many analysts have said, if Watergate had been just the June 1972 break-in at the Democratic headquarters in Washington, it would be little remembered today. If the Republican presidential reelection committee had immediately admitted its connection with the break-in's overzealous operatives, and apologized, a momentary political scandal would have faded away. Instead, an insistence on covering up sent the leadership of the United States into a whirlpool of deceit, with results that threatened the stability and future of the nation.

The cover-up, and the relationships among the Watergate participants, may be best understood in terms of the structure of power. Atop the power pyramid was Richard M. Nixon. A lawyer first elected to Congress in 1946, Nixon became nationally prominent as vice president during President Dwight D. Eisenhower's two terms (1953–60). Nixon then won the Republican presidential nomination, but lost a close election to John F. Kennedy. Two years later, he lost a race to become governor of California. But in 1968 he finally won the presidency and subsequently cruised to reelection in 1972. He was a man of pragmatically sweeping vision, as demonstrated by his improvement of the US position relative to the country's two superpower rivals, China and the Soviet Union (now Russia). He was also a man of meanness, suspicion, and deception, known to his foes as Tricky Dick.

The next-most-powerful men in the Nixon White House were two of his appointees, H.R. (Bob) Haldeman and John Ehrlichman. Neither had much political experience. Haldeman had been an advertising executive and Ehrlichman was a lawyer. Together they controlled access to the president, and Nixon trusted them with matters large and small, commendable and illegal. They were efficient. Haldeman, with his brusque manner and tight haircut, had the image of a Marine drill instructor. Ehrlichman at times appeared even more ruthless and cynical, though also creative in policy matters.

As the foreign policy expert, Henry Kissinger ranked equal to domestic adviser Ehrlichman, but Kissinger was much less a part of Nixon's inner circle and so, fortunately for him, relatively uninvolved in Watergate.

Down one level in the power structure were more lawyers. As the cover-up of the Watergate break-in became increasingly difficult to manage, Nixon relied heavily on the White House counsel, John W. Dean III, who was at first fearfully loyal to the president but who later testified against him. There was also the president's personal attorney, Herbert W. Kalmbach, and the attorney general, Richard Kleindienst, who went along with the plot, though with less enthusiasm than some.

During 1972 an allied power center was the Committee to Re-Elect the President, headed by former attorney general John Mitchell, also a lawyer. Nixon, after losing the California election, had gone to work in the same New York law firm as Mitchell, and Mitchell then went with Nixon to Washington after the 1968 election victory. The stern and dour Mitchell became known as the ultimate Nixon loyalist. In 1972 Mitchell supervised a reelection campaign that had far more money than usual and, it turned out, far wilder operatives. Mitchell may or may not have ordered the actual Watergate break-in, but he was later convicted of trying to cover it up and served nineteen months in jail. The same trial convicted

Haldeman (who served eighteen months in jail) and Ehrlichman (also eighteen months).

Mitchell's top deputy was Jeb Stuart Magruder, whose background was in advertising and merchandising. He became deputy director of communications in the White House in 1969, and then moved to the reelection committee. Smooth and personable, Magruder was an administration favorite until shortly before April 1973, when he began cooperating with federal prosecutors. Admitting his Watergate role, Magruder served seven months in jail.

Magruder had direct, if shadowy, supervision over the two men who ran the Watergate break-in team, E. Howard Hunt and G. Gordon Liddy. Hunt, an author and former CIA agent, and Liddy, a lawyer who had worked for the FBI, became operatives for the Nixon reelection committee. Hunt was "totally self-absorbed, totally amoral and a danger to himself and anybody around him," said former ambassador Samuel F. Hart, according to the *New York Times*. Liddy was even more of a loose cannon, plotting schemes that would have been outlandish even for movie scenarios while casting himself as an officer of self-discipline. Afterward, Hunt served almost three years in prison and Liddy more than four years.

Another loose cannon was Charles W. Colson, whose title was special counsel to the president, but whose chief duty seemed to be making life hard for Nixon's opponents, often unethically. Colson once declared he would "walk over my own grandmother" to make sure Nixon was reelected. As a result of Watergate, Colson served seven months in jail for obstructing justice.

These were the main Watergate conspirators—mostly lawyers, a few from a marketing background, and almost all with little political experience. The lawyers involved knew the law well, and yet were quite willing to break the law; it was not adherence to the law but rather another characteristic of the profession that these men emphasized, and that was lawyer as advocate. They believed their cause was more important than the rules. And though they portrayed their cause as what was best for the country, at heart and under pressure the cause was their craving for power.

The men who should have stopped them early on—the leaders of the FBI—did not step up forthrightly. The acting director of the FBI, L. Patrick Gray III, bowed to White House pressure by secretly destroying Watergate documents and by passing FBI files on to Dean. The FBI's second in command, W. Mark Felt, who had expected to run the agency, was quiet publicly but became the main secret source (known as Deep Throat) for the *Washington Post*'s extraordinarily thorough reporting on Watergate.

In contrast, special prosecutor Archibald Cox stood up for what was right. He stood so unwaveringly that Nixon had him fired. Also steadfast in the face of presidential power was a US District Court judge, John J. Sirica, who presided over the trials resulting from the Watergate charges; Earl J. Silbert, an assistant US attorney who insisted on going ahead with the prosecutions; and Sam J. Ervin Jr., chairman of a US Senate committee appointed to look into Watergate. Ervin—at turns pontifical, folksy, and dead-on—ran the hearings that paraded most of the cover-up participants in front of a national TV audience.

Critics were impatient with the pace of the investigation. More than two years passed between the break-in and when Nixon was essentially forced to resign, and another four months passed until his top aides were convicted. Then, when Gerald R. Ford, who became president when Nixon quit, suddenly pardoned Nixon before he could be put on trial—saying such action was for the good of the nation—critics asked why Nixon was not punished for defying the Constitution.

In this national drama of justice, fear, and abuse of power, twenty-five people went to jail. The facts and viewpoints that follow in this book illuminate the issues of a most extraordinary era.

World Map

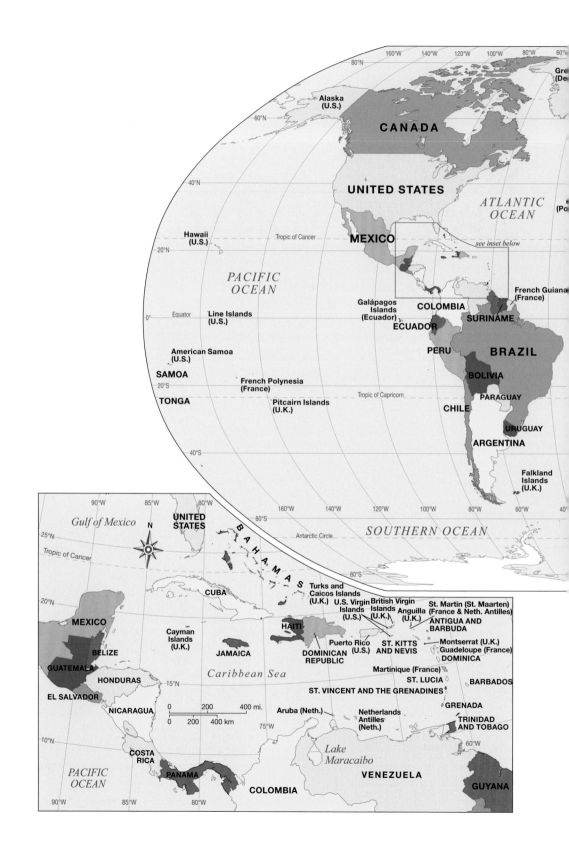

160°W   140°W   120°W   100°W   80°W   60°W

80°N

Greenland
(Denmark)

Alaska
(U.S.)

60°N

CANADA

ATLANTIC
OCEAN

40°N

UNITED STATES

(Portugal)

see inset below

Hawaii
(U.S.)

Tropic of Cancer

MEXICO

20°N

PACIFIC
OCEAN

French Guiana
(France)

Equator

Line Islands
(U.S.)

Galápagos
Islands
(Ecuador)

COLOMBIA

SURINAME

0°

ECUADOR

American Samoa
(U.S.)

PERU

BRAZIL

SAMOA

French Polynesia
(France)

BOLIVIA

20°S

Tropic of Capricorn

PARAGUAY

TONGA

Pitcairn Islands
(U.K.)

CHILE

URUGUAY

ARGENTINA

40°S

Falkland
Islands
(U.K.)

160°W   140°W   120°W   100°W   80°W   60°W   40°

60°S

Antarctic Circle

SOUTHERN OCEAN

80°S

90°W   85°W   80°W

Gulf of Mexico   N

UNITED
STATES

25°N

Tropic of Cancer

B A H A M A S

CUBA

Turks and
Caicos Islands
(U.K.)

U.S. Virgin
Islands
(U.S.)

British Virgin
Islands
(U.K.)

Anguilla
(U.K.)

St. Martin (St. Maarten)
(France & Neth. Antilles)
ANTIGUA AND
BARBUDA

20°N

MEXICO

Cayman
Islands
(U.K.)

HAITI

JAMAICA

Puerto Rico
(U.S.)

ST. KITTS
AND NEVIS

Montserrat (U.K.)
Guadeloupe (France)
DOMINICA

BELIZE

DOMINICAN
REPUBLIC

Martinique (France)

GUATEMALA

Caribbean Sea

ST. LUCIA

BARBADOS

HONDURAS

15°N

ST. VINCENT AND THE GRENADINES

EL SALVADOR

0   200   400 mi.

Aruba (Neth.)

Netherlands
Antilles
(Neth.)

GRENADA

NICARAGUA

0   200   400 km

TRINIDAD
AND TOBAGO

75°W

60°W

10°N

COSTA
RICA

Lake
Maracaibo

PACIFIC
OCEAN

PANAMA

VENEZUELA

GUYANA

COLOMBIA

90°W   85°W   80°W

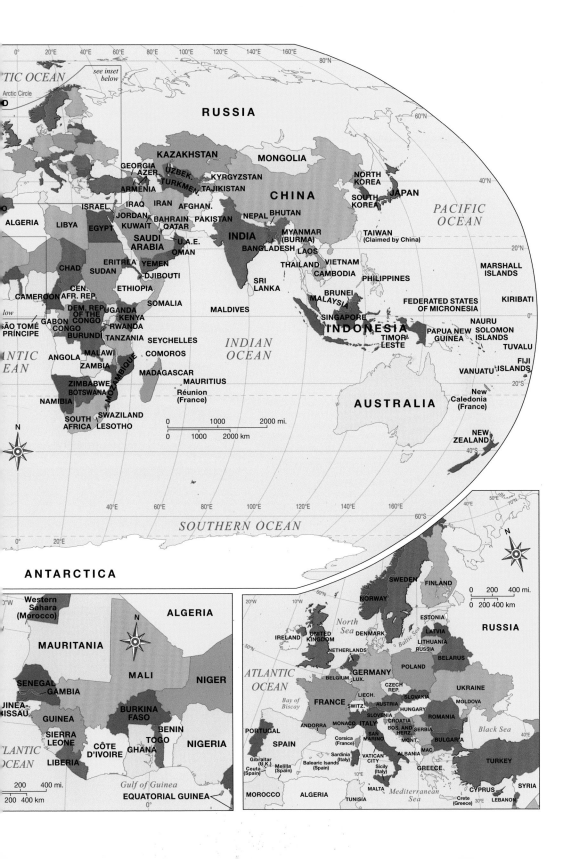

CHAPTER 1
Historical Background on Watergate

An Overview of Watergate, from the Break-In to the Resignation

Richard M. Flanagan and Louis W. Koenig

President Richard M. Nixon and his Republican associates were so afraid of possible defeat in the 1972 elections that they authorized shady and even illegal acts, including a break-in at the Democratic Party national headquarters at the Watergate complex, according to the authors of the following overview. The break-in failed and became public knowledge, and the Nixon administration's attempts to cover up its involvement in that and other schemes eventually backfired. After months of growing national controversy, administration resistance, US Senate hearings, and a US House committee's impeachment vote, Nixon resigned from the presidency. Richard M. Flanagan is an associate professor of political

Photo on previous page: The Watergate, which comprises office and apartment towers and a hotel, is located on the banks of the Potomac River in Washington, D.C. A scandal related to politically motivated burglaries at the complex led to President Richard Nixon's resignation. (© **Blaine Harrington III/ Corbis.**)

SOURCE. Richard M. Flanagan and Louis W. Koenig, *Dictionary of American History, 3E.* Charles Scribner's Sons, 2003, pp. 425–428. Copyright © 2003 by Global Rights & Permissions, a part of Cengage Learning, Inc. All rights reserved. Reproduced by permission. www .cengage.com/permissions.

science at City University of New York. Louis W. Koenig, a professor of government at New York University, has written several books about US presidents.

T he largest scandal of Richard M. Nixon's presidency unfolded with the burglary on 17 June 1972 of the Democratic National Committee headquarters in the Watergate apartment-office complex in Washington, D.C. The burglars were employees of the Committee for the Re-election of the President (CRP, called "CREEP" by Nixon's opponents) and were supervised by members of the White House staff. Watergate came to symbolize the efforts of the Nixon administration to subvert the democratic order through criminal acts; the suppression of civil liberties; the levying of domestic warfare against political opponents through espionage and sabotage, discriminatory income tax audits, and other punitive executive sanctions; and attempted intimidation of the news media. President Nixon's direct role in White House efforts to cover up involvement in the Watergate break-in was revealed in a tape of a 23 June 1972 conversation with White House chief of staff H.R. Haldeman, in which Nixon discussed a plan to have the CIA pressure the FBI to cease investigation of the Watergate case by claiming that national security secrets would be threatened if the Bureau widened its investigations. It was after this so-called "smoking gun" tape was made public on 6 August 1974 that President Nixon resigned from office on 9 August 1974.

The Beginnings

Watergate's roots can be traced to White House disappointment with the 1970 congressional elections. Fears that they foretold Nixon's possible defeat in 1972 were aggravated by massive antiwar demonstrations in Washington in 1971. These demonstrations were similar, the

Nixon White House believed, to those that had brought down Lyndon B. Johnson's presidency. In an atmosphere of a state of siege, White House special counsel Charles W. Colson developed a list of enemies, including several hundred persons from various walks of life. To cope with the menaces it perceived, the administration recruited undercover agents and made plans for domestic surveillance.

After leaks to the press had led to news accounts, in May 1969, of secret American air bombing raids in neutral Cambodia, the telephones of reporters and of the staff aides of Henry A. Kissinger, then national security assistant to the president, were wiretapped. The White House was further jarred by the publication in June 1971 in *The New York Times* and other newspapers of the "Pentagon Papers," a confidential Defense Department study of decision-making in the Vietnam War. In response, the White House increased the number of operatives trained in security and intelligence and established a "plumbers" unit to prevent "leaks." The Plumbers included E. Howard Hunt Jr., a former CIA agent, and G. Gordon Liddy, a former assistant district attorney in Dutchess County, New York. To secure information to prosecute or discredit Daniel Ellsberg, who had released the "Pentagon Papers," Hunt and other operatives in September 1971 broke into the office of Lewis Fielding, Ellsberg's psychiatrist, where they photographed records and papers.

> During the early presidential primaries the Plumbers and their hirelings engaged in espionage and sabotage.

In the first quarter of 1972, CRP raised unprecedented sums, from which various White House individuals, including Liddy, could draw directly. During the early presidential primaries the Plumbers and their hirelings engaged in espionage and sabotage against the candidacy of Senator Edmund S. Muskie, then considered the strongest potential Democratic presidential nominee. After Muskie's campaign foundered, similar activities were perpetrated against the two remaining leading candidates, Senator George McGovern, the eventual nominee, and Senator Hubert H. Humphrey. Liddy and others devised plans to disrupt the national Democratic convention and, through various contrived acts, to identify McGovern's candidacy with hippies, homosexuals, and draft evaders.

In January 1972 Attorney General John N. Mitchell, White House counsel John W. Dean III, and Jeb Stuart Magruder, an aide to White House Chief of Staff H.R. Haldeman and, in actuality, the chief administrator of CRP, attended a meeting held at the Justice Department. At that meeting Liddy presented a $1 million budgeted plan for electronic surveillance, photography of documents, and other activities for the approaching campaign. The plan was rejected as too expensive. At a second meeting in February, Liddy presented a revised plan and reduced budget. The approved plan centered on bugging Democratic National Committee headquarters at the Miami convention as well as the headquarters of the eventual Democratic presidential nominee. But the top priority target was the Democratic National Committee's headquarters at the Watergate complex in Washington and especially the office of the chairman, Lawrence R. O'Brien, whom the White House regarded as the Democrats' most professional political operative and a formidable competitor.

On the night of 27 May 1972, Liddy, Hunt, and James W. McCord Jr., another former CIA operative who had joined the Plumbers, along with a six-man group—chiefly Cuban exiles from Miami led by a former Hunt associate, Bernard L. Barker—taped doors leading to the Democratic headquarters, wiretapped the telephones in the offices, stole some documents, and photographed

Photo on following page: Ralph Metcalfe, a Democratic US representative from Illinois, holds a petition from his district with more than ten thousand names calling for the impeachment of President Nixon in May 1974. (Hulton Archive/ Getty Images).

others. They subsequently monitored the bugs while making futile attempts to break into McGovern's Washington headquarters. Since one tap had been placed improperly in the initial break-in, a Plumbers team returned to the Watergate Democratic headquarters on 17 June. Frank Wills, a security guard at the complex, noticed that some doors had been taped open and removed the tape. When he later returned and found doors retaped, he summoned the Washington police, and the five burglars, including McCord, were arrested and booked. E. Howard Hunt's White House telephone number was found on the person of two of the burglars, the first indication of White House involvement in the burglary.

The Cover-Up

A cover-up began (and never ended) in order to destroy incriminating evidence, obstruct investigations and, above all, halt any spread of scandal that might lead to the president. In his first public statement concerning Watergate on 29 August, Nixon declared that White House counsel John W. Dean III had "conducted a complete investigation of all leads" and had concluded that "no one in the White House staff" was "involved." Dean in fact coordinated the cover-up.

> A steady procession of White House aides and Justice Department officials resigned and were indicted, convicted . . . and imprisoned.

Hunt and four of the burglars pleaded guilty to all charges; McCord and Liddy stood trial and were convicted 30 January 1973 in the U.S. District Court of Judge John J. Sirica. Throughout the trial Sirica indicated that he believed that more than the seven men were involved. On 23 March, Sirica released a letter to him from McCord, in which McCord stated that higher-ups in CRP and the White House were involved, that the defendants had been pressured to plead guilty, and that perjury had been committed at the trial. The president repeatedly professed ignorance of CRP and White House involvement in Watergate. However, his claims were eventually challenged when specific aspects of his own conduct were revealed in criminal trials of his associates, in investigations by the Senate Watergate committee (chaired by Senator Sam Ervin), in staff studies by the House Judiciary Committee, and in tapes of White House conversations.

In statements before the Senate Watergate committee, Dean revealed that the president had promised clemency to Hunt and had said that it would be "no problem" to raise the "million dollars or more" necessary to keep Hunt and other defendants silent. In an address on 30 April 1973 the president accepted "responsibility" for the Watergate events but denied any advance knowledge of them or involvement in their cover-up. A steady procession of White House aides and Justice Department officials resigned and were indicted, convicted (including Mitchell, Dean, Haldeman, and John D. Ehrlichman), and imprisoned. Nixon himself was named an unindicted coconspirator by the federal grand jury in the Watergate investigation, and the U.S. Supreme Court allowed that finding to stand. Relentless probing by Special Watergate Prosecutor Archibald Cox led Nixon to order his firing. Both Attorney General Elliot Richardson and Deputy Attorney General William Ruckelshaus resigned, refusing to carry out Nixon's order. Robert H. Bork, the new Acting Attorney General, fired Cox. Leon Jaworski, Cox's successor, and the House Judiciary Committee, which considered impeachment of the president, were repeatedly rebuffed in requests for tapes and other evidence.

The impeachment charges that were ultimately brought against the president asserted that he had engaged in a "course of conduct" designed to obstruct justice in the Watergate case, and that in establishing the Plumbers and through other actions and inaction, he had failed to uphold the law. On 9 August 1974, faced with imminent impeachment, Nixon resigned as president. On 8 September 1974 his successor, Gerald R. Ford, pardoned Nixon for all federal crimes he "committed or may have committed or taken part in" while in office.

From the time of his resignation to his death in April 1994 Richard Nixon devoted much of his energy to rescuing his reputation from the long shadow of Watergate. For many Americans, acceptance of Ford's pardon by Nixon brought the presumption of felony guilt. Nixon fought attempts to make public his papers as well as the Watergate tapes. In public forums after his resignation Nixon minimized the ethical and legal misconduct of his staff and himself, focusing attention instead on the political context that led to his resignation. In 1990 Nixon's benefactors opened the Richard Nixon Library and Birthplace in Yorba Linda, California, without the benefit of the president's official papers, which are held, by act of Congress, in the Maryland facilities of the National Archives and Records Administration. After Nixon's death the tapes were made public and revealed an extensive pattern of Nixon's personal involvement and criminal action in Watergate.

News of a Break-In at the Watergate

Alfred E. Lewis

The public first learned of the Nixon administration's attempt to spy on Democratic Party leadership through the following report in the *Washington Post*. The article had substantial details about the break-in at the Watergate complex in Washington, D.C., and the arrests of five men, including a former CIA employee. The suspects carried almost $2,300, mostly in $100 bills, as well as espionage equipment. Their presence in the building was first detected by a young security guard who noticed doorway locks had been taped open and called the police. The following report is the complete original account. During fifty years as a reporter for the *Washington Post*, Alfred E. Lewis wrote more than 15,000 news articles, most of them involving the police.

Five men, one of whom said he is a former employee of the Central Intelligence Agency, were arrested at 2:30 A.M. yesterday in what authorities described as an elaborate plot to bug the offices of the Democratic National Committee here.

Three of the men were native-born Cubans and another was said to have trained Cuban exiles for guerrilla activity after the 1961 Bay of Pigs invasion.

They were surprised at gunpoint by three plain-clothes officers of the metropolitan police department in a sixth floor office at the plush Watergate, 2600 Virginia Ave., NW, where the Democratic National Committee occupies the entire floor.

> There was no immediate explanation as to why the five suspects would want to bug the Democratic National Committee offices.

There was no immediate explanation as to why the five suspects would want to bug the Democratic National Committee offices or whether or not they were working for any other individuals or organizations.

A spokesman for the Democratic National Committee said records kept in those offices are "not of a sensitive variety" although there are "financial records and other such information."

Police said two ceiling panels in the office of Dorothy V. Bush, secretary of the Democratic Party, had been removed.

Her office is adjacent to the office of Democratic National Chairman Lawrence F. O'Brien. Presumably, it would have been possible to slide a bugging device through the panels in that office to a place above the ceiling panels in O'Brien's office.

All wearing rubber surgical gloves, the five suspects were captured inside a small office within the committee's headquarters suite.

Police said the men had with them at least two sophisticated devices capable of picking up and transmitting all talk, including telephone conversations. In addition, police found lock-picks and door jimmies, almost

$2,300 in cash, most of it in $100 bills with the serial numbers in sequence.

The men also had with them one walkie-talkie, a short wave receiver that could pick up police calls, 40 rolls of unexposed film, two 35 millimeter cameras and three pen-sized tear gas guns.

Near where they were captured were two open file drawers, and one national committee source conjectured that the men were preparing to photograph the contents.

Five Suspects Are Identified

In court yesterday, one suspect said the men were "anti-Communists" and the others nodded agreement. The operation was described in court by prosecutor Earl J. Silbert as "professional" and "clandestine." One of the Cuban natives, *The Washington Post* learned, is now a Miami locksmith.

Many of the burglary tools found at the Democratic National Committee offices appeared to be packaged in what police said were burglary kits.

The five men were identified as:

- Edward Martin, alias James W. McCord, of New York City and perhaps the Washington metropolitan area. Martin said in court yesterday that he retired from the CIA two years ago. He said he presently is employed as a "security consultant."

- Frank Sturgis of 2515 NW 122d St., Miami. Prosecutors said that an FBI check on Sturgis showed that he had served in the Cuban Military army intelligence in 1958, recently traveled to Honduras in Central America, and presently is the agent for a Havana salvage agency. He has a home and family in Miami. Sturgis also was once charged with a gun violation in Miami, according to FBI records.

- Eugenio R. Martinez of 4044 North Meridian Ave., Miami. Prosecutors said that Martinez violated the immigration laws in 1958 by flying in a private plane to Cuba. He is a licensed real estate agent and a notary public in Florida.

- Virgilio R. Gonzales [editor's note: Spelling was corrected in subsequent stories to Gonzalez] of 930 NW 23d Ave., Miami. In Miami yesterday, his wife told a *Washington Post* reporter that her husband works as a locksmith at the Missing Link Key Shop. Harry Collot, the shop owner, said that Gonzales was scheduled to work yesterday but didn't show up. "He's done it before, but it's not a regular thing," Collot said. He said he thought Gonzales came to America about the time Fidel Castro became well-known, and began working for Missing Links sometime in 1959. He described Gonzales as "pro-American and anti-Castro . . . he doesn't rant or rave like some of them do."

- Bernard L. Barker of 5229 NW 4th St., Miami. Douglas Caddy, one of the attorneys for the five men, told a reporter that shortly after 3 A.M. yesterday, he received a call from Barker's wife. "She said that her husband told her to call me if he hadn't called her by 3 A.M.: that it might mean he was in trouble."

> All were charged with felonious burglary and with possession of implements of crime.

All were charged with felonious burglary and with possession of implements of crime. All but Martin were ordered held in $50,000 bail. Martin, who has ties in the area, was held in $30,000 bail.

In court yesterday, prosecutors said Sturgis also used the alias Frank Fiorini—an assertion confirmed by Miami area police.

In 1959, the Federal Aviation Agency identified Fiorini as the pilot of a plane that dropped anti-Castro leaflets over Havana. Described in newspaper clippings as a "soldier of fortune," Fiorini reportedly was head of

Frank Wills was the security guard who dis-covered the break-in at the Democratic Party offices. **(AP Photo.)**

the International Anticommunist Brigade, after the Bay of Pigs invasion, that trained 23 Cuban exiles who in 1962 landed by boat in Cuba's Matanzas Province and set up guerrilla operations.

(Fiorini reportedly is a native of Norfolk, Va., who fought with the Marines in the Pacific during World

PRESIDENTIAL APPROVAL RATINGS

At the time of the Watergate break-in, before anything was known about it, 59 percent of the American people approved of the job Richard Nixon was doing as president. The first chart shows his approval ratings at four-month intervals from the time of his second inauguration until just before his resignation. The second chart shows his highest and lowest approval ratings compared with those of the two presidents before and after Nixon.

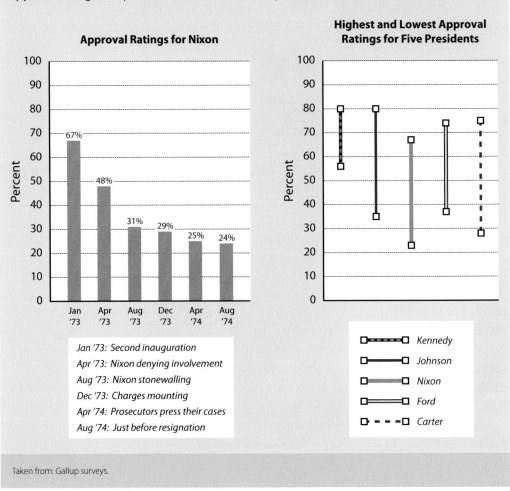

Jan '73: Second inauguration
Apr '73: Nixon denying involvement
Aug '73: Nixon stonewalling
Dec '73: Charges mounting
Apr '74: Prosecutors press their cases
Aug '74: Just before resignation

Taken from: Gallup surveys.

War II. An early supporter of the Cuban revolution, he reportedly fought with Castro and was named by the premier to be overseer of gambling operations in Havana before the casinos were shut down by the premier.)

Door Locks Had Been Taped

The early morning arrests occurred about 40 minutes after a security guard at the Watergate noticed that a door connecting a stairwell with the hotel's basement garage had been taped so it would not lock.

The guard, 24-year-old Frank Wills, removed the tape, but when he passed by about 10 minutes later a new piece had been put on. Wills then called police.

Three officers from the tactical squad responded and entered the stairwell.

From the basement to the sixth floor, they found every door leading from the stairwell to a hallway of the building had been taped to prevent them from locking. At the sixth floor, where the stairwell door leads directly into the Democratic National Committee offices, they found the door had been jimmied.

Led by Sgt. Paul Leper, the tactical force team, which also included Officers John Barret and Carl Shollfer, began searching the suite, which includes 29 offices and where approximately 70 persons work.

> One of the bugging devices found at the scene . . . was described as being about the size of a silver dollar.

When the officers entered an office occupied by a secretary to Stanley Griegg, deputy party chairman, one of the suspects jumped up from behind a desk, put his hands in the air and cried "don't shoot," police said.

According to police and a desk clerk at the Watergate, four of the suspects—all using fictitious names—rented two rooms, number 214 and 314 at the Watergate Hotel around noon on Friday. They were said to have dined together on lobster at the Watergate Restaurant on Friday night.

Yesterday afternoon, the U.S. Attorney's office obtained warrants to search the hotel rooms rented by the suspects. They found another $4,200 in $100 bills of the same serial number sequence as the money taken from the suspects, more burglary tools and electronic bugging equipment stashed in six suitcases.

One of the bugging devices found at the scene of the Democratic National Committee offices was described as being about the size of a silver dollar and capable of being hidden underneath a telephone or a desk.

According to police, the break-in at the Democratic National Committee offices yesterday was the third incident there since May 28.

On that date, according to police, an attempt was made to unscrew a lock on the door between 11 P.M. and 8 A.M.

According to one police source, at least some of the suspects registered as guests at the Watergate Hotel on that date.

On June 7, police said, a safe at the Committee headquarters was reported broken into and $100 in cash and checks stolen. That break-in occurred about 9 P.M. but there was no door jimmied since the suite was unlocked and people were still working there.

Within hours after the arrests, the suite was sealed off and scores of metropolitan police officers [arrived], directed by acting Chief Charles Wright. FBI agents and Secret Service men were assigned to the investigation.

The Five Are Taken to Court

Caddy, one of the attorneys for the five, said he met Barker a year ago over cocktails at the Army Navy Club in Washington. "We had a sympathetic conversation— that's all I'll say," Caddy told a reporter.

Caddy said that he was probably the only attorney whom Barker knew in Washington.

Caddy, who says he is a corporate lawyer, attempted to stay in the background of yesterday's 4 P.M. court hearing. He did not argue before Superior Court Judge James A. Belson himself but brought another attorney, Joseph

A. Rafferty Jr., who has experience in criminal law, to do the arguing.

In that 30-minute arraignment, Assistant U.S. Attorney Earl Silbert, the No. 2 man in the chief prosecutor's office, unsuccessfully urged the court to order the five men held without bond.

Silbert argued that the men had no community ties and would be likely to leave the country to avoid trial. He said they gave false names to the police after they were arrested and refused to cooperate.

"They were caught red-handed," Silbert said. With such strong evidence against them, their apparent tendency to travel abroad and their access to large amounts of cash, the men should not be released, Silbert said.

Silbert called the men professionals with a "clandestine" purpose.

Rafferty said the five men didn't have firearms and didn't harm anyone, and should be released on bond.

In setting the bond at $50,000 for the Miami men and $30,000 for Martin, Judge Belson also placed restrictions on their movements.

He required the four Miami men to stay in the Washington area and check in daily with the court, if released. Martin would have to check in weekly if released, Belson ruled.

Griegg, deputy party chairman, called it "obviously important" that some of the suspects come from the area around Miami and Miami Beach, where the Democratic National Convention will be held next month.

The *Washington Post* Reveals the Scandal, and the White House Fires Back

J. Anthony Lukas

As soon as the Watergate break-in became public, one of the first things President Richard Nixon did was deploy his top aides in a campaign to deflect the press, according to the author of the following excerpt. The administration's intimidation of journalists went on for the next two and a half years, but failed to squelch two young reporters for the *Washington Post*, Carl Bernstein and Bob Woodward. The two, who were quite different in personality and background from each other, managed to document and reveal connections between the break-in and the top levels of the president's reelection committee as well as the White House itself. J. Anthony Lukas was a Pulitzer Prize-winning journalist and author.

SOURCE. J. Anthony Lukas, "Uncover," in *Nightmare: The Underside of the Nixon Years*, The Viking Press, 1976, pp. 270–274. Copyright © 1976 by J. Anthony Lukas. All rights reserved. Reproduced by permission of SLL/Sterling Lord Literistic, Inc.

For decades, Richard Nixon treated the press with a contempt that lightly disguised roiling resentment. William Safire, the former public-relations man who served as a White House speechwriter, recalls Nixon's saying over and over again, "The press is the enemy." Indeed, if the Kennedy clan was the first of "them" and Dan Ellsberg later a close second, the press was the source of their special power to wound him. John Kennedy, in particular, had positively glimmered in the mirror of an adoring press, which never wearied of describing his "grace," "charm," "easy wit," and "boyish good looks." But to Nixon, the small-town boy who grew up listening to train whistles in the night, Kennedy was a rebuke to everything he stood for: hard work, perseverance, preparation, the old-style virtues which earned you rewards in the American system. As Nixon saw it, Kennedy never had to work for what he got; he just fooled the press into giving it to him. And Nixon, to whom nothing ever came easily, loathed the press for never trusting or loving him too.

Another man, settling luxuriously behind the desk in the Oval Office, might have abandoned or at least relaxed this grim vendetta. But not Nixon, particularly not after the fall of 1969 when the press pummeled his appointment of Clement F. Haynsworth, Jr., to the Supreme Court, assailed his hard line on Vietnam, and ridiculed his November 3 appeal to "the great Silent Majority of my fellow Americans." Instead, he gave the go-ahead for a speech [Vice President] Spiro Agnew gave on November 13 in Des Moines which blistered the "dozen anchormen, commentators, and executive producers [who] . . . decide what forty to fifty million Americans will learn of the day's events in the nation and in the world . . . read the

> There was . . . a special glee in Nixon's determination to bring the press to heel.

same newspapers . . . draw their political and social views from the same sources . . . talk constantly to one another, thereby providing artificial reinforcement to their shared viewpoint." Safire says Nixon went through the speech line by line in advance with its author, Pat Buchanan, toughened it in a few places, and then chortled, "This really flicks the scab off, doesn't it?"

The Denials Included Lies

For the next two and a half years Nixon kept up his campaign of intimidation against the press. He rewarded a few friendly reporters with exclusive interviews or tips, while ordering his aides to avoid all contact with critical journals like *The New York Times* or *St. Louis Post-Dispatch*. Reporters who dared to ask tough questions at news conferences—like Stuart Loory of the *Los Angeles Times*—abruptly found their access to White House officials cut off. All administrations do this kind of thing from time to time, but there was a special animus, a special glee in Nixon's determination to bring the press to heel.

Not surprisingly, then, one of the President's first steps following the Watergate break-in was to discuss with Bob Haldeman on June 20 [1972] ways of keeping the true story from the press and diverting their attention with a "PR offensive to top this." The day before, his press secretary, Ronald Ziegler, had refused to comment on what he called "a third-rate burglary attempt." On the twentieth, John Mitchell declared that CREEP [the Committee to Re-Elect the President] had not authorized the Watergate burglary and therefore was "not legally, morally, or ethically accountable for actions taken without its knowledge and beyond the scope of its control." At a news conference on June 22 the President echoed these statements, insisting that "the White House has no involvement whatever in this particular incident." And on August 29 these early denials were capped when

the President announced that John Dean had conducted "a complete investigation" of the Watergate affair—an outright fabrication, for there had been no such investigation—and determined that "no one in the White House staff, no one in this administration presently employed was involved in this very bizarre incident."

Some White House officials tried to mislead reporters by suggesting that the burglary was the work of anti-Castro Cubans—out to prove that the Democrats were getting contributions from Castro. The Washington *Evening Star*, which often followed the White House lead, went for the Cuban Connection completely, reporting in its July 7 edition that the break-in had been financed by "a right-wing group" of Cuban exiles. And *The New York Times* assigned the Watergate story at first to its Latin American specialist, Tad Szulc, who spent valuable days

Bob Woodward (right) and Carl Bernstein, reporting for the *Washington Post,* uncovered connections between the Watergate break-ins and Nixon's White House. (**AP Photo.**)

tracking down the ties Bernie Barker and his men had to Cuban exile groups in Miami.

Meanwhile, over at *The Washington Post* the story was being handled chiefly by two young metropolitan desk reporters, Carl Bernstein and Bob Woodward.

An Unlikely Pair Teams Up

"Woodstein"—as the reporting team came to be known—was a bizarre hybrid, a kind of journalistic centaur with an aristocratic Republican head and runty Jewish hindquarters. Bob Woodward was a tall, good-looking Yale graduate whose face *Vogue* magazine was later to call "as open as a Finnish sandwich." The son of a Midwestern judge, he had been a Naval officer for five years, drove a 1970 Karmann Ghia, and reminded Bernstein of "lawns, greensward, staterooms, and grass tennis courts." Bernstein was a rumpled, pock-marked, shaggy-haired dropout from the University of Maryland who occasionally wrote about rock music for the *Post* and reminded Woodward of "those counterculture journalists [he] despised." When they found themselves sharing the Watergate story in the days after the break-in, they were mutually suspicious and resentful. But soon they found that they worked well together: Woodward supplying the establishment credentials, the informed sources within government, a well-honed intelligence, and dogged diligence; Bernstein providing the writing skill, cunning, combativeness, and an almost feral intensity. They had other advantages for this kind of story. Woodward had recently been divorced, Bernstein was separated from his wife, so neither had a family life to prevent them from working twelve to eighteen hours a day, seven days a week. Both were ambitious young men—Woodward was twenty-nine, Bernstein was twenty-eight—who felt their talents were not fully recognized or utilized by the *Post*. (Woodward, on the paper barely nine months, had been relegated to minor police stories; Bernstein, in six years with the *Post*, had worked himself up from copyboy to the not terribly exalted job of Virginia political reporter.) Most important, they were outside the well-grooved orbit of big-time National Journalism, which seduced so many of its practitioners into a cozy rapport with their sources and a slothful delectation of their prestige and perquisites. Woodstein was a hungry animal that prowled through the back alleys of Washington journalism, feeding on the scraps

> Woodstein [Bob Woodward and Carl Bernstein] was a hungry animal that prowled through the back alleys of Washington journalism.

and gutter detritus, ignored by the well-tailored denizens of the National Press Club bar and the Sans Souci restaurant. Woodward had one supersource whom he called "Deep Throat" and met in drafty parking garages (and whom many believe to have been W. Mark Felt, Jr., then deputy associate director of the FBI). But most of their information was gleaned from less glamorous founts—bank records, telephone bills, crisscross directories, and the hazy recollections of secretaries, clerks, and minor officials whom they tracked through endless telephone calls and waited for on doorsteps in the middle of the night. "You know," a *Post* reporter told Timothy Crouse of *Rolling Stone*, "if that story had been given to our national staff, we probably would have lost it. These were two city-side guys with nothing to lose and they just worked their asses off."

At first, their labors brought only a meager harvest of minor exclusives—[E. Howard] Hunt's consultant status at the White House or his interest in Ted Kennedy. Then they began bringing down some riper fruit—snatched from a growing roster of disaffected sources: Hugh Sloan, the renegade campaign treasurer; a finance committee bookkeeper who realized ruefully that "something is rotten in Denmark and I'm part of it"; a few FBI agents

In 1976, Watergate Was Movie Magic

The movie *All the President's Men*, based on the book of the same title by Carl Bernstein and Bob Woodward, came out in 1976 and was a big hit. Telling the Watergate story with subtlety and power, it won critical acclaim, large audiences, and four Oscars, including best supporting actor for Jason Robards as *Washington Post* editor Ben Bradlee. The youthful Dustin Hoffman and Robert Redford starred as Bernstein and Woodward.

As happens in movies, *All the President's Men* compressed what happened in real life and presented it more dramatically, but there was enough truth to inspire both budding and veteran journalists for years to come.

Universities suddenly found their journalism classes were overflowing, and students went around quoting what the movie's Bradlee told Woodward and Bernstein after they discovered the extent of the Nixon administration's involvement in the cover-up: "Nothing's riding on this except the First Amendment of the Constitution, freedom of the press, and maybe the future of this country."

fed up with Pat Gray; or Justice Department officials dismayed at the cover-up.

And from August through October, Woodstein produced a spate of "scoops" which changed the shape of the Watergate story for good: August 1—the Dahlberg check and the financial link between CREEP and the Watergate burglary; September 16—the "secret fund" controlled by Maurice Stans and CREEP aides; September 17—Jeb Magruder's and Bart Porter's withdrawals from the fund;

September 29—Mitchell's control of the fund; and on October 10 a blockbuster which wove together the various strands of their investigation into a story which began: "F.B.I. agents have established that the Watergate bugging incident stemmed from a massive campaign of political spying and sabotage conducted on behalf of President Nixon's re-election and directed by officials of the White House and the Committee for the Re-election of the President." In that and subsequent stories they also revealed Donald Segretti's activities; his ties to Dwight Chapin, Gordon Strachan, and Herb Kalmbach; and Ken Clawson's alleged admission that he had written the "Canuck" letter.

> "The President took the *Post*'s reporting as a personal affront.

The White House Fires Back

The President took the *Post*'s reporting as a personal affront. On September 15 Dean told him," . . . the *Post*, as you know, has got a real large team that they've assigned to do nothing but this," and Nixon said, "The *Post* is going to have damnable, damnable problems out of this one. They have a television station." (They had several stations, all subject to license challenges before the Federal Communications Commission. Within months, three challenges had been filed against WJXT in Jacksonville, and another against WPLG in Miami. Both stations were owned by the *Post*. The challenges were not successful, but there is strong evidence to indicate that they were instigated by the Nixon administration.)

The administration fought back more publicly too, with scathing denunciations of the *Post*'s stories: "a collection of absurdities," "a senseless pack of lies," "shabby journalism," "unfounded and unsubstantiated allegations," "mud-slinging," "guilt by association," "a political effort by *The Washington Post*, well conceived and coordinated, to discredit this administration and individuals in it," "using innuendo, third-person hearsay, unsubstantiated charges, anonymous sources, and huge scare headlines, the *Post* has maliciously sought to give the appearance of a direct connection between the White House and the Watergate."

The US House of Representatives Issues the Articles of Impeachment

Judiciary Committee of the US House of Representatives

As president, Richard M. Nixon obstructed justice, violated the rights of citizens, and defied lawful requests for information by the US House of Representatives—actions that are not permitted by the Constitution, according to the legislators' Judiciary Committee. Nixon should face a trial in the Senate on those three kinds of charges the committee concluded in its indictment, known as an impeachment. The committee's vote was 27–11, and the majority included six Republicans. Nixon's lawbreaking included using presidential powers for widespread deceit and subversion. The committee's vote came two years and one month after the Watergate break-in. The following entry is the complete articles of impeachment against Nixon.

SOURCE. Judiciary Committee, US House of Representatives, "Articles of Impeachment Against Richard M. Nixon," July 27, 1974.

RESOLVED, That Richard M. Nixon, President of the United States, is impeached for high crimes and misdemeanours, and that the following articles of impeachment to be exhibited to the Senate:

ARTICLES OF IMPEACHMENT EXHIBITED BY THE HOUSE OF REPRESENTATIVES OF THE UNITED STATES OF AMERICA IN THE NAME OF ITSELF AND OF ALL OF THE PEOPLE OF THE UNITED STATES OF AMERICA, AGAINST RICHARD M. NIXON, PRESIDENT OF THE UNITED STATES OF AMERICA, IN MAINTENANCE AND SUPPORT OF ITS IMPEACHMENT AGAINST HIM FOR HIGH CRIMES AND MISDEMEANOURS.

Article I

In his conduct of the office of President of the United States, Richard M. Nixon, in violation of his constitutional oath faithfully to execute the office of President of the United States and, to the best of his ability, preserve, protect, and defend the Constitution of the United States, and in violation of his constitutional duty to take care that the laws be faithfully executed, has prevented, obstructed, and impeded the administration of justice, in that:

On June 17, 1972, and prior thereto, agents of the Committee for the Re-election of the President committed unlawful entry of the headquarters of the Democratic National Committee in Washington, District of Columbia, for the purpose of securing political intelligence. Subsequent thereto, Richard M. Nixon, using the powers of his high office, engaged personally and through his close subordinates and agents, in a course of conduct or plan designed to delay, impede, and obstruct the investigation of such illegal entry; to cover up, conceal and protect those

> Richard M. Nixon . . . has prevented, obstructed, and impeded the administration of justice.

responsible; and to conceal the existence and scope of other unlawful covert activities.

The means used to implement this course of conduct or plan included one or more of the following:

1. making false or misleading statements to lawfully authorized investigative officers and employees of the United States;

2. withholding relevant and material evidence or information from lawfully authorized investigative officers and employees of the United States;

In August 1974, US representatives listen to the White House tapes that reveal President Nixon's participation in the Watergate scandal. **(Hulton Archive/ Getty Images.)**

3. approving, condoning, acquiescing in, and counselling witnesses with respect to the giving of false or misleading statements to lawfully authorized investigative officers and employees of the United States and false or misleading testimony in duly instituted judicial and congressional proceedings;

4. interfering or endeavouring to interfere with the conduct of investigations by the Department of Justice of the United States, the Federal Bureau of Investigation, the office of Watergate Special Prosecution Force, and Congressional Committees;

5. approving, condoning, and acquiescing in, the surreptitious payment of substantial sums of money for the purpose of obtaining the silence or influencing the testimony of witnesses, potential witnesses or individuals who participated in such unlawful entry and other illegal activities;

6. endeavouring to misuse the Central Intelligence Agency, an agency of the United States;

7. disseminating information received from officers of the Department of Justice of the United States to subjects of investigations conducted by lawfully authorized investigative officers and employees of the United States, for the purpose of aiding and assisting such subjects in their attempts to avoid criminal liability;

8. making or causing to be made false or misleading public statements for the purpose of deceiving the people of the United States into believing that a thorough and complete investigation had been conducted with respect to allegations of misconduct on the part of personnel of the executive branch of the United States and personnel of the Committee for the Re-election of the President, and that there was no involvement of such personnel in such misconduct: or

9. endeavouring to cause prospective defendants, and individuals duly tried and convicted, to expect favoured treatment and consideration in return for their silence or false testimony, or rewarding individuals for their silence or false testimony.

In all of this, Richard M. Nixon has acted in a manner contrary to his trust as President and subversive of constitutional government, to the great prejudice of the cause of law and justice and to the manifest injury of the people of the United States.

Wherefore Richard M. Nixon, by such conduct, warrants impeachment and trial, and removal from office.

Article II

Using the powers of the office of President of the United States, Richard M. Nixon, in violation of his constitutional oath faithfully to execute the office of President of the United States and, to the best of his ability, preserve, protect, and defend the Constitution of the United States, and in disregard of his constitutional duty to take care that the laws be faithfully executed, has repeatedly engaged in conduct violating the constitutional rights of citizens, impairing the due and proper administration of justice and the conduct of lawful inquiries, or contravening the laws governing agencies of the executive branch and the purposed of these agencies.

This conduct has included one or more of the following:

1. He has, acting personally and through his subordinates and agents, endeavoured to obtain from the Internal Revenue Service, in violation of the constitutional rights of citizens, confidential information contained in income tax returns for purposed not authorized by law, and to cause, in violation of the constitutional rights of citizens, income tax audits

A Long-Secret Recording Sealed Nixon's Fate

Six days after the burglars were arrested in the Watergate offices of the Democratic National Committee, Richard Nixon had a conversation with his chief of staff, H.R. (Bob) Haldeman. They talked about how to thwart an FBI investigation of the Watergate break-in, because the FBI would probably discover the connection between the burglary and the White House.

Haldeman suggested having the deputy director of the CIA tell the FBI chief to stay out of the situation because it involved Cuba and CIA national security operations; some of the arrested men were Cubans.

Nixon responded: "All right. Fine."

The highly detailed conversation proved Nixon was aware of the Watergate plot and helped to cover it up—facts that he and his associates would deny for the next two years. The conversation, on July 23, 1972, was recorded on the automatic taping system in Nixon's office, but it was kept secret as Nixon went on to win reelection. Finally, on August 5, 1974, after the special prosecutor's office finally obtained the tape, the transcript was made public. Nixon resigned as president four days later.

or other income tax investigations to be initiated or conducted in a discriminatory manner.

2. He misused the Federal Bureau of Investigation, the Secret Service, and other executive personnel, in violation or disregard of the constitutional rights of citizens, by directing or authorizing such agencies or personnel to conduct or continue electronic surveillance or other investigations for purposes unrelated

to national security, the enforcement of laws, or any other lawful function of his office; he did direct, authorize, or permit the use of information obtained thereby for purposes unrelated to national security, the enforcement of laws, or any other lawful function of his office; and he did direct the concealment of certain records made by the Federal Bureau of Investigation of electronic surveillance.

> In disregard of the rule of law, [Nixon] knowingly misused the executive power.

3. He has, acting personally and through his subordinates and agents, in violation or disregard of the constitutional rights of citizens, authorized and permitted to be maintained a secret investigative unit within the office of the President, financed in part with money derived from campaign contributions, which unlawfully utilized the resources of the Central Intelligence Agency, engaged in covert and unlawful activities, and attempted to prejudice the constitutional right of an accused to a fair trial.

4. He has failed to take care that the laws were faithfully executed by failing to act when he knew or had reason to know that his close subordinates endeavoured to impede and frustrate lawful inquiries by duly constituted executive, judicial and legislative entities concerning the unlawful entry into the headquarters of the Democratic National Committee, and the cover-up thereof, and concerning other unlawful activities including those relating to the confirmation of Richard Kleindienst as Attorney General of the United States, the electronic surveillance of private citizens, the break-in into the offices of Dr. Lewis Fielding, and the campaign financing practices of the Committee to Re-elect the President.

5. In disregard of the rule of law, he knowingly misused the executive power by interfering with agencies of the executive branch, including the Federal Bureau of Investigation, the Criminal Division, and the Office of Watergate Special Prosecution Force, of the Department of Justice, and the Central Intelligence Agency, in violation of his duty to take care that the laws be faithfully executed.

In all of this, Richard M. Nixon has acted in a manner contrary to his trust as President and subversive of constitutional government, to the great prejudice of the cause of law and justice and to the manifest injury of the people of the United States.

Wherefore Richard M. Nixon, by such conduct, warrants impeachment and trial, and removal from office.

Article III

In his conduct of the office of President of the United States, Richard M. Nixon, contrary to his oath faithfully to execute the office of President of the United States and, to the best of his ability, preserve, protect, and defend the Constitution of the United States, and in violation of his constitutional duty to take care that the laws be faithfully executed, has failed without lawful cause or excuse to produce papers and things as directed by duly authorized subpoenas issued by the Committee on the Judiciary of the House of Representatives on April 11, 1974, May 15, 1974, May 30, 1974, and June 24, 1974, and willfully disobeyed such subpoenas. The subpoenaed papers and things were deemed necessary by the Committee in order to resolve by direct evidence fundamental, factual questions relating to Presidential direction, knowledge or approval of actions demonstrated by other evidence to be substantial grounds for impeachment of the President. In refusing to produce these papers and things Richard M. Nixon, substituting his judgment as to what materials were necessary for the inquiry, interposed the powers of the Presidency against the lawful subpoenas of the House of Representatives, thereby assuming to himself functions and judgments necessary to the exercise of the sole power of impeachment vested by the Constitution in the House of Representatives.

In all of this, Richard M. Nixon has acted in a manner contrary to his trust as President and subversive of constitutional government, to the great prejudice of the cause of law and justice, and to the manifest injury of the people of the United States.

Wherefore, Richard M. Nixon, by such conduct, warrants impeachment and trial, and removal from office.

President Nixon Announces His Resignation

Richard M. Nixon

The President preferred to remain in office and fight the charges against him, but his political base had become too weak, he told the people of the United States in his speech of resignation. To continue the battle would disrupt the nation at a time when it needed to address the needs of peace overseas and prosperity at home, he declared. He said he hoped citizens would unite in supporting the new president, Gerald Ford, and that the United States would begin an era of healing. The President admitted some mistaken judgments, but did not acknowledge lawbreaking or directly address the issues of Watergate. He cited substantial achievements during his time in office, particularly in relationships with other countries. The following is his complete resignation speech. Richard M. Nixon was the thirty-seventh president of the United States.

SOURCE. Richard M. Nixon, "Address to the Nation Announcing Decision to Resign the Office of President of the United States," *The American Presidency Project*, August 8, 1974.

Good evening:

This is the 37th time I have spoken to you from this office, where so many decisions have been made that shaped the history of this Nation. Each time I have done so to discuss with you some matter that I believe affected the national interest.

In all the decisions I have made in my public life, I have always tried to do what was best for the Nation. Throughout the long and difficult period of Watergate, I have felt it was my duty to persevere, to make every possible effort to complete the term of office to which you elected me.

In the past few days, however, it has become evident to me that I no longer have a strong enough political base in the Congress to justify continuing that effort. As long as there was such a base, I felt strongly that it was necessary to see the constitutional process through to its conclusion, that to do otherwise would be unfaithful to the

> " I have never been a quitter. "

spirit of that deliberately difficult process and a dangerously destabilizing precedent for the future.

But with the disappearance of that base, I now believe that the constitutional purpose has been served, and there is no longer a need for the process to be prolonged.

I would have preferred to carry through to the finish, whatever the personal agony it would have involved, and my family unanimously urged me to do so. But the interests of the Nation must always come before any personal considerations.

From the discussions I have had with Congressional and other leaders, I have concluded that because of the Watergate matter, I might not have the support of the Congress that I would consider necessary to back the very difficult decisions and carry out the duties of this office in the way the interests of the Nation will require.

I have never been a quitter. To leave office before my term is completed is abhorrent to every instinct in my body. But as President, I must put the interests of America first. America needs a full-time President and a full-time Congress, particularly at this time with [the] problems we face at home and abroad.

To continue to fight through the months ahead for my personal vindication would almost totally absorb the time and attention of both the President and the Congress in a period when our entire focus should be on the great issues of peace abroad and prosperity without inflation at home.

Therefore, I shall resign the Presidency effective at noon tomorrow. Vice President [Gerald] Ford will be sworn in as President at that hour in this office.

America Needs Unity

As I recall the high hopes for America with which we began this second term, I feel a great sadness that I will not be here in this office working on your behalf to achieve those hopes in the next 2 ½ years. But in turning over direction of the Government to Vice President Ford, I know, as I told the Nation when I nominated him for that office 10 months ago, that the leadership of America will be in good hands.

In passing this office to the Vice President, I also do so with the profound sense of the weight of responsibility that will fall on his shoulders tomorrow and, therefore, of the understanding, the patience, the cooperation he will need from all Americans.

As he assumes that responsibility, he will deserve the help and the support of all of us. As we look to the future, the first essential is to begin healing the wounds of this Nation, to put the bitterness and divisions of the recent past behind us and to rediscover those shared ideals that lie at the heart of our strength and unity as a great and as a free people.

Photo on previous page: President Nixon says goodbye outside the White House on August 9, 1974, after his resignation. (Rolls Press/Popperfoto/Getty Images.)

By taking this action, I hope that I will have hastened the start of that process of healing which is so desperately needed in America.

I regret deeply any injuries that may have been done in the course of the events that led to this decision. I would say only that if some of my judgments were wrong—and some were wrong—they were made in what I believed at the time to be the best interest of the Nation.

> I leave with no bitterness toward those who have opposed me.

To those who have stood with me during these past difficult months—to my family, my friends, to many others who joined in supporting my cause because they believed it was right—I will be eternally grateful for your support.

And to those who have not felt able to give me your support, let me say I leave with no bitterness toward those who have opposed me, because all of us, in the final analysis, have been concerned with the good of the country, however our judgments might differ.

So, let us all now join together in affirming that common commitment and in helping our new President succeed for the benefit of all Americans. I shall leave this office with regret at not completing my term, but with gratitude for the privilege of serving as your President for the past 5 ½ years. These years have been a momentous time in the history of our Nation and the world. They have been a time of achievement in which we can all be proud, achievements that represent the shared efforts of the administration, the Congress, and the people.

Great Challenges Await the United States

But the challenges ahead are equally great, and they, too, will require the support and the efforts of the Congress and the people working in cooperation with the new Administration.

We have ended America's longest war, but in the work of securing a lasting peace in the world, the goals ahead are even more far-reaching and more difficult. We must complete a structure of peace so that it will be said of this generation, our generation of Americans, by the people of all nations, not only that we ended one war but that we prevented future wars.

We have unlocked the doors that for a quarter of a century stood between the United States and the People's Republic of China.

We must now ensure that the one quarter of the world's people who live in the People's Republic of China will be and remain not our enemies, but our friends.

In the Middle East, 100 million people in the Arab countries, many of whom have considered us their enemy for nearly 20 years, now look on us as their friends. We must continue to build on that friendship so that peace can settle at last over the Middle East and so that the cradle of civilization will not become its grave.

Together with the Soviet Union, we have made the crucial breakthroughs that have begun the process of limiting nuclear arms. But we must set as our goal not just limiting but reducing and, finally, destroying these terrible weapons so that they cannot destroy civilization and so that the threat of nuclear war will no longer hang over the world and the people.

We have opened the new relation with the Soviet Union. We must continue to develop and expand that new relationship so that the two strongest nations of the world will live together in cooperation, rather than confrontation.

Around the world in Asia, in Africa, in Latin America, in the Middle East, there are millions of people who live in terrible poverty, even starvation. We must keep as our goal turning away from production for war and expanding production for peace so that people everywhere on this Earth can at last look forward in their children's

> I have fought for what I believed in. I have tried, to the best of my ability, to discharge [my] duties.

time, if not in our own time, to having the necessities for a decent life.

Here in America, we are fortunate that most of our people have not only the blessings of liberty but also the means to live full and good and, by the world's standards, even abundant lives. We must press on, however, toward a goal, not only of more and better jobs but of full opportunity for every American and of what we are striving so hard right now to achieve, prosperity without inflation.

A Dedication to the Cause of Peace

For more than a quarter of a century in public life, I have shared in the turbulent history of this era. I have fought for what I believed in. I have tried, to the best of my ability, to discharge those duties and meet those responsibilities that were entrusted to me.

Sometimes I have succeeded and sometimes I have failed, but always I have taken heart from what Theodore Roosevelt once said about the man in the arena, "whose face is marred by dust and sweat and blood, who strives valiantly, who errs and comes short again and again because there is not effort without error and shortcoming, but who does actually strive to do the deed, who knows the great enthusiasms, the great devotions, who spends himself in a worthy cause, who at the best knows in the end the triumphs of high achievements and who at the worst, if he fails, at least fails while daring greatly."

I pledge to you tonight that as long as I have a breath of life in my body, I shall continue in that spirit. I shall continue to work for the great causes to which I have been dedicated throughout my years as a Congressman, a Senator, Vice President, and President, the cause of peace, not just for America but among all nations—prosperity, justice, and opportunity for all of our people.

There is one cause above all to which I have been devoted and to which I shall always be devoted for as long as I live.

When I first took the oath of office as President 5 ½ years ago, I made this sacred commitment: to "consecrate my office, my energies, and all the wisdom I can summon to the cause of peace among nations."

> All of our children have a better chance than before of living in peace rather than dying in war.

I have done my very best in all the days since to be true to that pledge. As a result of these efforts, I am confident that the world is a safer place today, not only for the people of America but for the people of all nations, and that all of our children have a better chance than before of living in peace rather than dying in war.

This, more than anything, is what I hoped to achieve when I sought the Presidency. This, more than anything, is what I hope will be my legacy to you, to our country, as I leave the Presidency.

To have served in this office is to have felt a very personal sense of kinship with each and every American. In leaving it, I do so with this prayer: May God's grace be with you in all the days ahead.

President Ford Pardons Nixon

Gerald R. Ford

The national interest compelled a pardon for Richard Nixon, his successor declared to the nation. In a brief speech, the recently installed president says he is issuing the pardon before Nixon could face a trial because the process of going through the courts would take years and would disrupt the country. Besides, he says, Nixon had already undergone the unique penalty of resigning from the nation's highest office. Ford puts his emphasis on a sense of fairness and conveys a need to move on. The following is the complete speech granting the pardon. Gerald R. Ford was the thirty-eighth president of the United States. He became vice president by appointment, after Spiro Agnew's resignation, and became president through Nixon's departure.

SOURCE. Gerald R. Ford, "Granting Pardon to Richard Nixon," The Watergate Files, September 8, 1974.

Richard Nixon became the thirty-seventh President of the United States on January 20, 1969 and was reelected in 1972 for a second term by the electors of forty-nine of the fifty states. His term in office continued until his resignation on August 9, 1974.

Pursuant to resolutions of the House of Representatives, its Committee on the Judiciary conducted an inquiry and investigation on the impeachment of the President extending over more than eight months. The hearings of the Committee and its deliberations, which received wide national publicity over television, radio, and in printed media, resulted in votes adverse to Richard Nixon on recommended Articles of Impeachment.

As a result of certain acts or omissions occurring before his resignation from the Office of President, Richard Nixon has become liable to possible indictment and trial for offenses against the United States. Whether or not he shall be so prosecuted depends on findings of the appropriate grand jury and on the discretion of the authorized prosecutor. Should an indictment ensue, the accused shall then be entitled to a fair trial by an impartial jury, as guaranteed to every individual by the Constitution.

It is believed that a trial of Richard Nixon, if it became necessary, could not fairly begin until a year or more has elapsed. In the meantime, the tranquility to which this nation has been restored by the events of recent weeks could be irreparably lost by the prospects of bringing to trial a former President of the United States. The prospects of such trial will cause prolonged and divisive debate over the propriety of exposing to further punishment and degradation a man who has already paid the unprecedented penalty of relinquishing the highest elective office of the United States.

> The tranquility to which this nation has been restored . . . could be irreparably lost by the prospects of bringing to trial a former President of the United States.

NOW, THEREFORE, I, Gerald R. Ford, President of the United States, pursuant to the pardon power conferred upon me by Article II, Section 2, of the Constitution, have granted and by these presents do grant a full, free, and absolute pardon unto Richard Nixon for all offenses against the United States which he, Richard Nixon, has committed or may have committed or taken part in during the period from January 20, 1969 through August 9, 1974.

IN WITNESS WHEREOF, I have hereunto set my hand this eighth day of September, in the year of our Lord nineteen hundred and seventy-four, and of the Independence of the United States of America the one hundred and ninety-ninth.

CHAPTER 2

Controversies Surrounding Watergate

Watergate Was an Extraordinarily Serious Set of Crimes

Sam J. Ervin Jr.

The following viewpoint is an excerpt from the report by the US Senate committee that investigated Watergate and held public hearings questioning many of the people involved. In it, the chairman charges that Richard Nixon and his appointees in the White House and political allies in the Republican Party tried to destroy the integrity of the presidential election process and to conceal their unethical and illegal acts. Although they took in immense amounts of cash from corporations, they were not seeking riches but instead lusted for power, he says. That lust blinded them to the laws of the United States as well as the laws of God, the senator concluded. To prevent such scandals in the future, citizens must elect officials who are dedicated to the public good and who have high moral and intellectual character. Sam J. Ervin Jr. was a

Photo on previous page: A window display in New York shows some of the public's attitude toward the Watergate scandal. (Joe Schilling/Time & Life Pictures/Getty Images.)

SOURCE. Sam J. Ervin Jr., "Individual Views of Senators of the Select Committee," *Final Report of the Senate Select Committee on Presidential Campaign Activities*, US Government Printing Office, 1974, pp. 1097–1103.

Democratic US senator from North Carolina for twenty years and chaired the Senate Select Committee on Presidential Campaign Activities.

Since the Senate Select Committee on Presidential Campaign Activities is filing with the Senate its final report concerning the investigation that body authorized and directed it to make, I deem it appropriate to state as succinctly as possible some of my personal observations respecting the tragic events known collectively as the Watergate, which disgraced the Presidential election of 1972.

In doing this, I ask and endeavor to answer these questions: What was Watergate? Why was Watergate? Is there an antidote which will prevent future Watergates? If so, what is that antidote?

Before attempting to answer these questions, I wish to make these things plain:

1. I am not undertaking to usurp and exercise the power of impeachment, which the Constitution confers upon the House of Representatives alone. As a consequence, nothing I say should be construed as an expression of an opinion in respect to the question of whether or not President Nixon is impeachable in connection with the Watergate or any other matter.

2. Inasmuch as its Committee on the Judiciary is now studying whether or not it ought to recommend to the House the impeachment of the President, I shall also refrain from making any comment on the question of whether or not the President has performed in an acceptable manner his paramount constitutional obligation "to take care that the laws be faithfully executed."

> Watergate was unprecedented in the political annals of America in respect to the scope and intensity of its unethical and illegal actions.

3. Watergate was not invented by enemies of the Nixon administration or even by the news media. On the contrary, Watergate was perpetrated upon America by White House and political aides, whom President Nixon himself had entrusted with the management of his campaign for reelection to the Presidency, a campaign which was divorced to a marked degree from the campaigns of other Republicans who sought election to public office in 1972. I note at this point without elaboration that these White House and political aides were virtually without experience in either Government or politics apart from their association with President Nixon.

4. Life had not subjected these White House and political aides to the disadvantaged conditions which are glibly cited as the causes of wrongdoing. On the contrary, fortune had smiled upon them. They came from substantial homes, possessed extraordinary talents, had had unusual educational opportunities, and occupied high social positions.

5. Watergate was unprecedented in the political annals of America in respect to the scope and intensity of its unethical and illegal actions. To be sure, there had been previous milder political scandals in American history. That fact does not excuse Watergate. Murder and stealing have occurred in every generation since Earth began, but that fact has not made murder meritorious or larceny legal.

What Was Watergate?

President Nixon entrusted the management of his campaign for reelection and his campaign finances to the Committee for the Re-Election of the President, which was headed by former Attorney General John N. Mitchell, and the Finance Committee to Re-Elect the President, which was headed by former Secretary of Commerce,

Maurice Stans. Since the two committees occupied offices in the same office building in Washington and worked in close conjunction, it seems proper to call them for ease of expression the Nixon reelection committees.

Watergate was a conglomerate of various illegal and unethical activities in which various officers and employees of the Nixon reelection committees and various White House aides of President Nixon participated in varying ways and degrees to accomplish these successive objectives:

1. To destroy, insofar as the Presidential election of 1972 was concerned, the integrity of the process by which the President of the United States is nominated and elected.

2. To hide from law enforcement officers, prosecutors, grand jurors, courts, the news media, and the American people the identities and wrongdoing of those officers and employees of the Nixon reelection committees, and those White House aides who had undertaken to destroy the integrity of the process by which the President of the United States is nominated and elected.

To accomplish the first of these objectives, the participating officers and employees of the reelection committees and the participating White House aides of President Nixon engaged in one or more of these things:

1. They exacted enormous contributions—usually in cash—from corporate executives by impliedly implanting in their minds the impressions that the making of the contributions was necessary to insure that the corporations would receive governmental favors, or avoid governmental disfavors, while President Nixon remained in the White House. A substantial portion of the contributions were made out of corpo-

Liddy Had Big Schemes, Mitchell Listened

G. Gordon Liddy, the Nixon administration employee who supervised the Watergate burglary team, had envisioned a much more extensive program against the Democrats in 1972, according to his autobiography, *Will*.

John Mitchell, the US attorney general and head of the Nixon reelection effort, invited Liddy to his office on January 27 to describe the plan. Liddy's proposals, budgeted at a total of $1 million, included: infiltrating spies into the campaign organizations of the Democratic presidential contenders; using a chase plane for electronic eavesdropping on the eventual Democratic nominee; secretly monitoring phone conversations; destroy-

ing the air-conditioning units while the Democrats were conducting their national convention in Miami that summer; secretly paying for outrageously provocative pro-Democrat demonstrators at the convention; and outfitting an opulent barge in Miami where beautiful young women would lure prominent Democrats for sexual escapades that would be recorded.

Mitchell, along with prominent associates, listened to all the proposals, Liddy noted, without raising any questions about their dubious legality. At the conclusion, Mitchell's only response to the plan was: It's too expensive. He added, "I'd like you to go back and come up with something more realistic."

rate funds in violation of a law enacted by Congress a generation ago.

2. They hid substantial parts of these contributions in cash in safes and secret deposits to conceal their sources and the identities of those who had made them.

3. They disbursed substantial portions of these hidden contributions in a surreptitious manner to finance the bugging and the burglary of the offices of the Democratic National Committee in the Watergate complex in Washington for the purpose of obtaining political intelligence; and to sabotage by dirty tricks,

espionage, and scurrilous and false libels and slanders the campaigns and the reputations of honorable men, whose only offenses were that they sought the nomination of the Democratic Party for President and the opportunity to run against President Nixon for that office in the Presidential election of 1972.

4. They deemed the departments and agencies of the Federal Government to be the political playthings of the Nixon administration rather than impartial instruments for serving the people, and undertook to induce them to channel Federal contracts, grants, and loans to areas, groups, or individuals so as to promote the reelection of the President rather than to further the welfare of the people.

> They deemed the departments and agencies of the Federal Government to be the political playthings of the Nixon administration.

5. They branded as enemies of the President individuals and members of the news media who dissented from the President's policies and opposed his reelection, and conspired to urge the Department of Justice, the Federal Bureau of Investigation, the Internal Revenue Service, and the Federal Communications Commission to pervert the use of their legal powers to harass them for so doing. . . .

Why Was Watergate?

Unlike the men who were responsible for Teapot Dome [a bribery scandal during US president Warren G. Harding's administration] the Presidential aides who perpetrated Watergate were not seduced by the love of money, which is sometimes thought to be the root of all evil. On the contrary, they were instigated by a lust for political power, which is at least as corrupting as political power itself.

They gave their allegiance to the President and his policies. They had stood for a time near to him, and had been entrusted by him with great governmental and political power. They enjoyed exercising such power, and longed for its continuance.

They knew that the power they enjoyed would be lost and the policies to which they adhered would be frustrated if the President should be defeated.

As a consequence of these things, they believed the President's reelection to be a most worthy objective, and succumbed to an age-old temptation. They resorted to evil means to promote what they conceived to be a good end.

> " They resorted to evil means to promote what they conceived to be a good end. "

Their lust for political power blinded them to ethical considerations and legal requirements; to Aristotle's aphorism that the good of man must be the end of politics; and to Grover Cleveland's conviction that a public office is a public trust.

They had forgotten, if they ever knew, that the Constitution is designed to be a law for rulers and people alike at all times and under all circumstances; and that no doctrine involving more pernicious consequences to the commonweal has ever been invented by the wit of man than the notion that any of its provisions can be suspended by the President for any reason whatsoever.

On the contrary, they apparently believed that the President is above the Constitution, and has the autocratic power to suspend its provisions if he decides in his own unreviewable judgment that his action in so doing promotes his own political interests or the welfare of the Nation. As one of them testified before the Senate Select Committee, they believed that the President has the autocratic power to suspend the Fourth Amendment whenever he imagines that some indefinable aspect of national security is involved.

I digress to reject this doctrine of the constitutional omnipotence of the President. As long as I have a mind to

A US Senate committee investigates the Watergate scandal on June 27, 1973. (Popperfoto/ Getty Images.)

think, a tongue to speak, and a heart to love my country, I shall deny that the Constitution confers any autocratic power on the President, or authorizes him to convert George Washington's America into Gaius Caesar's Rome.

The lust for political power of the Presidential aides who perpetrated Watergate on America blinded them to the laws of God as well as to the laws and ethics of man. . . .

The Antidote for Future Watergates

Is there an antidote which will prevent future Watergates? If so, what is it?

The Senate Select Committee is recommending the enactment of new laws which it believes will minimize the danger of future Watergates and make more adequate and certain the punishment of those who attempt to perpetrate them upon our country.

Candor compels the confession, however, that law alone will not suffice to prevent future Watergates. In saying this, I do not disparage the essential role which law plays in the life of our Nation. As one who has labored as a practicing lawyer, a judge, and a legislator all of my adult years, I venerate the law as an instrument of service to society. At the same time, however, I know the weakness of the law as well as its strength.

> Law alone will not suffice to prevent future Watergates.

Law is not self-executing. Unfortunately, at times its execution rests in the hands of those who are faithless to it. And even when its enforcement is committed to those who revere it, law merely deters some human beings from offending, and punishes other human beings for offending. It does not make men good. This task can be performed only by ethics or religion or morality.

Since politics is the art or science of government, no man is fit to participate in politics or to seek or hold public office unless he has two characteristics.

The first of these characteristics is that he must understand and be dedicated to the true purpose of government, which is to promote the good of the people, and entertain the abiding conviction that a public office is a public trust, which must never be abused to secure private advantage.

The second characteristic is that he must possess that intellectual and moral integrity, which is the priceless ingredient in good character.

When all is said, the only sure antidote for future Watergates is [the] understanding of fundamental principles and intellectual and moral integrity in the men and women who achieve or are entrusted with governmental or political power.

Josiah Gilbert Holland, a poet of a bygone generation, recognized this truth in a poem which he called "The Day's Demand," and which I like to call "America's Prayer." I quote his words:

> God give us men! A time like this demands
> Strong minds, great hearts, true faith and ready hands;
> Men whom the lust of office does not kill;
> Men whom the spoils of office cannot buy;
> Men who possess opinions and a will;
> Men who have honor—men who will not lie;
> Men who can stand before a demagogue
> And damn his treacherous flatteries without winking;
> Tall men, sun-crowned, who live above the fog
> In public duty, and in private thinking.

President Nixon Deserved to Be Removed from Office

Barbara Jordan

Reason, not passion, requires that Richard Nixon be impeached, according to the following opening statement as the US House Judiciary Committee began proceedings on whether to indict the president. It was delivered by a relatively young congresswoman whose ancestors were not allowed to vote because of their race. Those who would put off the question or who say the evidence is insufficient, she asserts, are not facing the facts. She cites statements of the country's founding fathers in contrast to Nixon administration lies. If the Constitution's impeachment provision is not invoked to impeach Nixon, she concludes, then the Constitution is worthless. Barbara Jordan was a Democratic member of the US House of Representatives for six years, part of a long career in public service.

SOURCE. Barbara Jordan, "Statement," Debate on Articles of Impeachment, *Hearings of the Committee on the Judiciary, House of Representatives*, US Government Printing Office, 1974, pp. 110–113.

Earlier today [July 25, 1974] we heard the beginning of the Preamble to the Constitution of the United States, "We, the people." It is a very eloquent beginning. But when that document was completed, on the seventeenth of September in 1787, I was not included in that "We, the people." I felt somehow for many years that George Washington and Alexander Hamilton just left me out by mistake. But through the process of amendment, interpretation, and court decision I have finally been included in "We, the people." Today I am an inquisitor. I believe hyperbole would not be fictional and would not overstate the solemnness that I feel right now. My faith in the Constitution is whole, it is complete, it is total. I am not going to sit here and be an idle spectator to the diminution, the subversion, the destruction of the Constitution. . . .

> I am not going to sit here and be an idle spectator to the diminution, the subversion, the destruction of the Constitution.

Common sense would be revolted if we engaged upon this process for petty reasons. Congress has a lot to do. Appropriations, tax reform, health insurance, campaign finance reform, housing, environmental protection, energy sufficiency, mass transportation. Pettiness cannot be allowed to stand in the face of such overwhelming problems. So today we are not being petty. We are trying to be big because the task we have before us is a big one.

This morning, in a discussion of the evidence, we were told that the evidence which purports to support the allegations of misuse of the CIA by the president is thin. We are told that that evidence is insufficient. What that recital of the evidence this morning did not include is what the president did know on June 23, 1972. The president did know that it was Republican money, that it was money from the Committee for the Re-Election of the President, which was found in the possession of one of the burglars arrested on June 17.

What the president did know on June 23 was the prior activities of E. Howard Hunt, which included his participation in the break-in of Daniel Ellsberg's psychiatrist [office], which included Howard Hunt's participation in the Dita Beard ITT affair, which included Howard Hunt's fabrication of cables designed to discredit the [John F.] Kennedy administration.

We were further cautioned today that perhaps these proceedings ought to be delayed because certainly there would be new evidence forthcoming from the president of the United States. There has not even been an obfuscated indication that this committee would receive any additional materials from the president. The committee subpoena is outstanding, and if the president wants to supply that material, the committee sits here.

The fact is that yesterday, the American people waited with great anxiety for eight hours, not knowing whether their president would obey an order of the Supreme Court of the United States.

Constitutional History Supports Impeachment

At this point I would like to juxtapose a few of the impeachment criteria with some of the president's actions.

Impeachment criteria: James Madison, from the Virginia ratification convention. "If the president be connected in any suspicious manner with any person and there be grounds to believe that he will shelter him, he may be impeached."

We have heard time and time again that the evidence reflects payment to the defendants of money. The president had knowledge that these funds were being paid and that these were funds collected for the 1972 presidential campaign.

We know that the president met with Mr. Henry Petersen [assistant attorney general] twenty-seven times to discuss matters related to Watergate and immediately

MS. JORDAN

Barbara Jordan, a member of the House Judiciary Committee, addresses fellow US representatives on July 25, 1974. (AP Photo.)

thereafter met with the very persons who were implicated in the information Mr. Petersen was receiving and transmitting to the president. The words are "if the president be connected in any suspicious manner with any person and there be grounds to believe that he will shelter that person, he may be impeached."

Justice [Joseph] Story: "Impeachment is intended for occasional and extraordinary cases where a superior power acting for the whole people is put into operation to protect their rights and rescue their liberties from violations."

We know about the Huston plan. We know about the break-in of the psychiatrist's office. We know that there was absolute complete direction in August 1971 when the president instructed [top aide John] Ehrlichman to "do whatever is necessary." This instruction led to a surreptitious entry into Dr. Fielding's office.

"Protect their rights." "Rescue their liberties from violation."

The South Carolina ratification convention impeachment criteria: those are impeachable "who behave amiss or betray their public trust."

Beginning shortly after the Watergate break-in and continuing to the present time, the president has engaged in a series of public statements and actions designed to thwart the lawful investigation by government prosecutors. Moreover, the president has made public announcements and assertions bearing on the Watergate case which the evidence will show he knew to be false.

> The president has engaged in a series of public statements and actions designed to thwart the lawful investigation.

These assertions, false assertions, impeachable, those who misbehave. Those who "behave amiss or betray their public trust."

James Madison again at the Constitutional Convention: "A president is impeachable if he attempts to subvert the Constitution."

The Constitution charges the president with the task of taking care that the laws be faithfully executed, and yet the president has counseled his aides to commit perjury, willfully disregarded the secrecy of grand jury proceedings, concealed surreptitious entry, attempted to compromise a federal judge while publicly displaying his cooperation with the processes of criminal justice.

"A president is impeachable if he attempts to subvert the Constitution."

If the impeachment provision in the Constitution of the United States will not reach the offenses charged here, then perhaps that eighteenth century Constitution should be abandoned to a twentieth-century paper shredder. Has the president committed offenses and planned and directed and acquiesced in a course of conduct which the Constitution will not tolerate? That is the question. We know that. We know the question. We should now forthwith proceed to answer the question. It is reason, and not passion, which must guide our deliberations, guide our debate, and guide our decision.

The Media Hated Nixon and Drove Him from Office

Patrick J. Buchanan

Richard Nixon won reelection by a landslide in 1972, a feat that infuriated a liberal media and political elite, a former adviser to Richard Nixon asserts in the following viewpoint. According to him, members of this elite despised Nixon because throughout his career in public service he had bravely shown them wrong about the New Deal, the Soviet government, the Vietnam War, and the existence of a "great silent majority" of Americans. While major newspapers were printing stolen defense documents, Nixon was trying to preserve national security. Nixon did abuse his power, he writes, but to no greater extent than previous Democratic presidents—presidents who were cheered on by the hypocrites of the left wing. Columnist, author, and public affairs analyst Patrick J. Buchanan was a senior adviser to three US presidents, including Nixon, and sought the presidency himself.

Until I saw an unctuous individual babbling on about how our terrified city feared a coup d'etat by Richard Nixon in 1974, I had decided not to write on the 25th anniversary of Watergate. But that did it. Watergate was indeed a coup. It was the overthrow of an elected president by a media and political elite he had routed in a 49-state landslide the like of which America had never seen.

In taking Nixon down, that elite was not motivated by any love of law or the Constitution. It was driven by hatred.

> "In taking Nixon down [the media and political] elite was not motivated by any love of law or the Constitution. It was driven by hatred."

The media and political establishment hated Nixon for his lead role in nailing Alger Hiss as a Soviet spy and in blistering its New Deal heroes as witless dupes of Joseph Stalin. It hated Nixon because he rallied the nation against them, when he called on the "Great Silent Majority" to stand with him for peace with honor in Vietnam, and turned Vice President [Spiro] Agnew loose on them to the delight of a nation that had come to detest media arrogance and bias. And it hated Nixon because he seemed, with the mining of Haiphong and bombing of Hanoi, to have won a war they said could not—and should not—be won.

With every provincial capital under Saigon control, and America's POWs coming home, the left seethed with resentment. And when it was revealed in March of 1973 that there had been a cover-up of the Watergate break-in, the establishment united as one to destroy Nixon. Nixon shredded the Constitution! they howled.

But this is arrant nonsense. The Constitution was in tatters when Nixon arrived in the capital in 1969. It had been scissored to bits by Earl Warren, William O. Douglas, William Brennan and the rest of the merry men of the Warren Court. And every unconstitutional power grab by that renegade court was celebrated by this city.

Nixon had an "Enemies List," they cried. How awful! But if anything terrible ever happened to anyone on that list—other than a lost invitation to a White House Christmas party—it has yet to be discovered.

Nixon abused the FBI to cover up Watergate, they said. Yep, he did try to keep the FBI from expanding the Watergate investigation into campaign finance. But earlier, many of the same journalists who professed themselves sickened by this "abuse of power" had been recipients of the fruits of the FBI surveillance of the hotel rooms of Martin Luther King Jr., with recordings and photos of King's liaisons provided, courtesy of

The *New York Times* resumed publication of its series of articles based on the secret Pentagon papers in its July 1, 1971, edition, after the US Supreme Court ruled in its favor. (**AP Photo/Jim Wells.**)

THE NEWS MEDIA SLIPS IN PUBLIC OPINION POLLS

The public's view of the credibility of mass news media has dropped since the 1970s, when Richard Nixon was in office. The chart below shows, for selected years, the percentages of Americans surveyed who said they had a great deal or fair amount of trust and confidence in the mass media's news reporting.

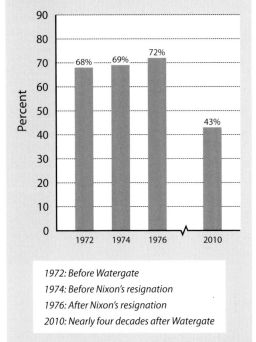

1972: Before Watergate
1974: Before Nixon's resignation
1976: After Nixon's resignation
2010: Nearly four decades after Watergate

Taken from: Gallup surveys.

Lyndon Johnson's White House. The press has never called to account the White House and Justice Department aides responsible. What did Nixon ever do to anyone, compared to what the liberals did to Dr. King?

Nixon tried to block the *New York Times* and the *Washington Post* from printing the Pentagon Papers! He sure did. To this day, I find nothing wrong with the elected head of the executive branch going to the Supreme Court to seek an injunction against publication of top-secret documents stolen from the U.S. Department of Defense by a disloyal employee.

The Pentagon Papers had nothing to do with Nixon. They detailed the decision-making of the [John F.] Kennedy and Johnson administrations, which had marched us into the Asian war from which Nixon was bravely trying to extricate the nation with honor. Yet, Nixon was bedeviled at every step by the same hypocrites who had cheered on JFK and LBJ.

Did Nixon misuse and abuse his power? Yes, he did. Instead of creating a "Plumbers" unit in the White House to run down national security leaks, he should have left the black-bag jobs, as his predecessors did, to J. Edgar Hoover. But Nixon was not hated so much for what he did wrong as for what he did right—exposing the near-treasonous conduct of much of the American Left during Vietnam.

And when his presidency was broken, that Left saw to it that aid to Vietnam was cut off, guaranteeing the defeat and death of the South in the all-out invasion by the Communist North in 1975. The mind-set of Nixon enemies was never more manifest than in their uncontrolled rage and hysteria when President [Gerald] Ford pardoned him, denying them the sensual delight of seeing Nixon in the dock. History, however, has a way of settling accounts.

Having destroyed Nixon, the liberals got Jimmy Carter, who announced that Vietnam was a "racist" war and Americans had gotten over our "inordinate fear of Communism." During Carter's one term, the Soviet empire drove deeper into Asia, Africa and even Central America, producing a conservative backlash that elected Ronald Reagan, who declared Vietnam "a noble cause" and led America to triumph in the Cold War. So let the Left celebrate how it saved us all from Richard Nixon, as the republic recalls who it was that rescued America from the Left and saved the world from the Soviet empire.

Executive Privilege Is a Disservice to Democracy

Raoul Berger

A democracy works only if its people have access to information and government officials are accountable to them, a legal scholar writes in the following viewpoint. So when a president insists on his or her own authority—executive privilege—to withhold information from Congress and the public at large, the country's future is at risk. The histories of the United States and of other nations have shown that collective judgment is more reliable than trusting in any one individual, he writes. Open debate may be messy and prolonged, and congressional investigations may sometimes be excessive, yet the alternative is a secrecy that can shield corruption and evil, he concludes. Raoul Berger, an attorney and professor, wrote eight books about the federal government and the US Constitution.

SOURCE. Raoul Berger, "Conclusion," in *Executive Privilege: A Constitutional Myth*, Cambridge, MA: Harvard University Press, 1974, pp. 344–347. Copyright © 1974 by the President and Fellows of Harvard College. Reprinted by permission of the publisher.

A democratic system rests on full access to information and accountability to the people. Speaking of an executive refusal to disclose conflicting
agency reports, Justice Potter Stewart said that, when
"the people and their representatives are reduced to ignorance the democratic process is paralyzed." Our Constitution provides for congressional participation "in the
great decisions that spell life and death to the Nation."
Meaningful participation is possible only on the basis of
full information; without knowledge of the alternatives
that have been spread before the President, and withheld
from Congress, legislative decisionmaking stumbles in
the dark. When based on full information, the participation of Congress insures that the issues will be aired
instead of being decided in a hall of mirrors where cour-
tiers echo the desires of the monarch.

With all its shortcomings, its fumbling, disorgani-
zation, susceptibility to manipulation, shrinking from
responsibility, Congress yet has one great redeeming
feature: it is the national forum of debate. Here ideas can
be tested in the crucible of open discussion; here debate
can bring into the open risks that executive advisers
have overlooked or underestimated; it may show that
the supposed advantages of a recommended course of
action are outweighed by the concomitant risks. At all
times there will be dissident voices, uncowed by a strong
presidential personality or by the current of popular
opinion. A George Norris, [William] Borah, [Robert]
La Follette, or Wayne Morse, like Winston Churchill in
the 1930's, will cry alarm. Debate also substitutes the
experience of the many for that of the one. The wise old
[Benjamin] Franklin, at the close of the Constitutional
Convention, adjured the strong-willed delegates to swal-
low their remaining differences on the assumption that
the collective judgment is more reliable than that of any
one member. Whether the people will be swayed is not
so important as that they should have the opportunity to

Attorney Raoul Berger (right)—seen here in his Washington, DC, office with automobile entrepreneur Preston Tucker in 1948—was an outspoken critic of executive privilege. (**AP Photo/William J. Smith.**)

hear opposition views, to have an informed choice of options, to be alerted to possible consequences of massive commitments rather than to have commitments saddled on them by secret one-man decisions. Above all, debate may serve to secure the consent of the people. A Vietnam war hawk, Senator John Stennis, speaking in favor of a bill that would require congressional authorization for the waging of war, said: "Vietnam has shown us that by trying to fight a war without the clear-cut prior support of the American people we may not only risk military ineffectiveness but we also strain, and can shatter, the very structure of the Republic."

Whatever the merits of debate, this is a requirement of a democratic society. Those who are to bleed and die have a right to be consulted, to have the issues debated by their elected representatives; for a nation of two hundred million cannot be convened in a town meeting. Unlike the totalitarian nations we have not placed our faith in a Fuehrer, a Big Brother; a benign dictatorship is not for us. "With all its defects, delays or inconveniences," said Justice [Robert H.] Jackson, "men have discovered no technique for long preserving free government except that the Executive be under the law, and that the law be made by parliamentary deliberations." Experience with strong royal authority, said Sir Denis Brogan, taught the English that the worst elected chamber was better than the best royal antechamber. That lesson should not be lost on the viewers who heard the testimony of the White House camarilla in the Watergate Hearings.

> He who controls the flow of information rules our destinies.

Against free congressional inquiry it is customary to pit the spectre of McCarthyism. But the spectacle of Senator [Joseph] McCarthy whip-lashing innocent victims [in his hunt for Communist infiltrators in the 1950s], revolting as it was, was not nearly so costly to the nation as the "escalation by stealth" in Vietnam or the conspiracy to corrupt the electoral process that burst upon our vision at Watergate. A generation so given to "balancing" competing policies should ask whether the occasional excesses of congressional investigations were as damaging to the nation as the evils which have flowed from unrestricted secrecy.

He who controls the flow of information rules our destinies. So much Vietnam alone should prove. It was not the design of the Founders that the people and the Congress should obtain only so much information as the President concluded was fitting for them to have. As a partner—the senior partner—in the conduct of our government, Congress is entitled to share *all* the information that pertains to its affairs. The basic presupposition of our society was the widest access to information except, in the words of John Marshall, when disclosure would be attended by "fatally pernicious" consequences. Given, as James Iredell said, that the officers of the government—the President included—are the "servants and agents of the people," it is a contradiction in terms to conclude that the agent may dole out information to his principal. The perils of that course were underscored by a great early American statesman, Edward Livingston:

> No nation ever yet found any inconvenience from too close an inspection into the conduct of its officers, but many have been brought to ruin, and . . . slavery . . . only because the means of publicity had not been secured.

Executive Privilege Is Constitutionally Validated

Mark J. Rozell

Properly used, executive privilege is not only a presidential necessity but is constitutionally correct, the author of the following selection contends. The problem has been that one president, Richard Nixon, abused his power, and so the practice of withholding certain information is now seen by some as evil. This circumstance has led to mutual suspicion among the branches of the federal government. Agreement as to when and how executive privilege is rightly used, he asserts, requires an understanding of the separation of powers doctrine. It is impossible to write precise rules for when the use of executive privilege is appropriate, so mutual respect is necessary in order to properly determine the legitimacy of such privilege. Mark J. Rozell, a professor of public policy at George Mason University, has written frequently about politics and the US presidency.

SOURCE. Mark J. Rozell, "Resolving the Dilemma," *Executive Privilege: The Dilemma of Secrecy and Democratic Accountability*, The Johns Hopkins University Press, 1994, pp. 142–147. Reproduced by permission.

The dilemma of executive privilege is that of permitting governmental secrecy in a political system predicated on leadership accountability. On the surface, the dilemma is a complex one to resolve: How can democratically elected leaders be held accountable by the public when they are able to deliberate in secret or to make secretive decisions?

The evidence shows that presidential exercise of the doctrine of executive privilege fits comfortably within the embrace of our constitutional system. That constitutional doctrine has evolved over the course of our history and traditionally has been accepted by the coordinate branches of government as a legitimate executive branch power.

Nonetheless, in more recent years, the doctrine of executive privilege has fallen into disrepute because of the leadership abuses of one presidency. Members of Congress consequently show little or no deference to presidential exercise of executive privilege. Presidential administrations seek various means for withholding information, oftentimes by disguising executive privilege. The pattern of executive branch recriminations against legislators for meddling where they don't belong and legislative branch accusations that executive branch failure to divulge all information constitutes criminal activity has been unhealthful to our governing system. Currently there appears to be a lack of recognition by the political branches of each other's legitimate powers and interests in the area of governmental secrecy. To restore some sense of comity and cooperation between the political branches on issues of executive branch secrecy, the following points must be recognized.

First, executive privilege is a legitimate constitutional doctrine validated by the writings of the constitutional Framers, broad residual executive powers contained in

> Not every assertion of executive privilege is automatically a devious attempt to conceal wrongdoing.

Article II of the Constitution, historical exercise, congressional acceptance, and judicial opinion. The weight of the evidence clearly refutes the assertion that executive privilege is a "constitutional myth." Consequently, presidential administrations should not be devising schemes for achieving the ends of executive privilege while avoiding any mention of the constitutional doctrine. Furthermore, Congress must recognize that the executive branch—like the legislative and judicial branches—has a legitimate need to deliberate in secret and that not every assertion of executive privilege is automatically a devious attempt to conceal wrongdoing.

Second, executive privilege is not an unlimited, unfettered presidential power. Executive privilege should

Supporters of President Nixon held a prayer vigil in July 1974 during the Watergate crisis. **(Keystone/Getty Images.)**

be exercised only rarely and for the most compelling reasons. Congress has the right—and often the duty—to challenge presidential assertions of executive privilege when such assertions clearly are not related to such legitimate needs as protecting national security or the candor of internal deliberations.

Third, there are no clear, precise constitutional boundaries that determine, a priori [prior to analysis or experience], whether any particular claim of executive privilege is legitimate. The resolution to the dilemma of executive privilege is found in the political ebb and flow of our separation of powers system. There is, in fact, no need for any precise definition of the constitutional boundaries surrounding executive privilege. Such a power cannot be subject to precise definition because it is impossible to determine in advance all of the circumstances under which presidents may have to exercise that power. A return to the traditional separation of powers theory provides the appropriate resolution to the dilemma of executive privilege and democratic accountability.

The Two Extremes of the Executive Privilege Debate

In response to such a constitutional dilemma as posed by presidential use of executive privilege, it is often tempting to try to devise a remedy that would eliminate any potential future conflict. The preeminent critic of executive privilege, Raoul Berger, believes that there is just one answer to the question of how to resolve this constitutional dilemma: eliminate the source of power from which the dilemma originates. In Berger's view, "secrecy in the operations of government is an abomination." Berger concludes that the case of the [Richard] Nixon presidency proves that point. Under the Nixon presidency, Berger writes, "'confidentiality' was the vehicle for the cover-up of criminal acts and conspiracies by

[Nixon's] aides, an instrument he repeatedly employed to the obstruction of justice."

Berger's assessment of Nixon's exercise of executive privilege is unarguable. Yet many of the critiques of executive privilege—within both Congress and the academic community—focus on the incredible abuses of a single presidency. Generalizing from the abuses of power in the Nixon White House, many critics of executive privilege maintain that, therefore, there must be completely open deliberations within the executive branch of government (a position never adopted even by the "open" presidencies of Gerald R. Ford or Jimmy Carter). These critics, while having identified an undeniable problem, call for simplistic, blanket solutions. That is, if such a power as executive privilege can potentially be abused, then it must be eliminated in favor of completely open, public deliberations. They perceive such openness as the only means by which to assure accountability from the executive branch.

Underlying this argument against executive privilege is the view that Congress must always be supreme in the lawmaking process given the need for democratic accountability and the specific powers conferred upon the legislative branch by Article I of the Constitution. Some scholars see no exceptions to that rule. Berger dismisses the existence of residual or prerogative powers for the president, even in foreign affairs and emergency situations. David Gray Adler argues that the Constitution makes Congress the supreme branch in the conduct of foreign policy and war. "The president is vested with only modest authority in this area and is clearly only of secondary importance." Adler maintains that the end of the Cold War eliminates any rationale for executive preeminence in foreign policy.

James W. Ceaser argues that the belief that Congress must always be supreme in the lawmaking process, even at the expense of tying the hands of the executive during

Many Presidents Have Used Executive Privilege

The term "executive privilege" was first used in the 1950s, but the concept—and controversy—began in the administration of the first president of the United States. What the term means is that the executive branch asserts it is entitled to keep certain information secret.

Since George Washington's time, US presidents have said that the national interest requires such secrecy and that members of the executive branch will not be fully open and honest in discussing possible policies if Congress and the courts can use their words against them. In the latter sense, executive privilege is like attorney-client or doctor-patient privilege: For an effective relationship, some things must be kept secret.

Over the years, presidents of both major US political parties have cited executive privilege, including a predecessor to Richard Nixon (a Republican). John F. Kennedy (a Democrat) did not allow his top military adviser to testify to a House of Representatives committee about a 1961 raid on Cuba.

The US Constitution does not include a presidential right to secrecy. The controversy over Nixon's assertions went to the US Supreme Court, which ruled in 1974 that the president may claim, in certain circumstances, a right of executive privilege. But the justices said the validity of the claim had to be decided in the court system, case by case.

times of emergency, "is based on a narrow and legalistic understanding of the Constitution and on a failure to recognize the real purpose for which the founders adopted the theory of separation of powers." The failure to understand or to accept the founders' theory of the separation of powers has resulted in the quest for absolutes on the issue of executive privilege. Modern-day congressionalists seek ways to deny presidential powers because such powers can be abused. The congressionalists subsequently elevate the exception—the abuse of power—into the rule, leading to the call for broad, sweeping solutions.

Many of former president Nixon's defenders, on the other hand, elaborated the equally suspect argument that Congress and the public have no authority to limit and constrain the exercise of executive powers. The extreme statement of this view was Nixon's claim that any action undertaken by the president is legitimate. Nixon's attorneys submitted the argument that how the executive privilege is exercised "is a matter of presidential judgment alone." In the case *U.S. v. Sirica* (1973), Judge George MacKinnon expressed best of all the notion of an unlimited executive privilege: "In my opinion an absolute privilege exists for presidential communications. . . . [S]trict confidentiality is so essential to the deliberative process that it should not be jeopardized by any possibility of disclosure."

> Only a proper understanding of the separation of powers doctrine can help resolve the inherent conflict.

Neither Side Is Right or Practical

Neither the congressional supremacy view nor the imperial presidency view presents an accurate assessment of the separation of powers system. Neither provides a workable resolution to the dilemma of executive privilege. Yet only a proper understanding of the separation of powers doctrine can help resolve the inherent conflict between governmental secrecy and the "right to know."

The alternative proposed by the congressional supremacists—completely open executive branch deliberations—is worse than the danger that they seek to eliminate. Any power once created can be abused. And because secrecy is vital to the proper functioning of the presidency, periodic attempts to abuse this power may be an unavoidable price that must be accepted. To demand that presidents exercise their powers fully to move forward an activist policy agenda, that they strictly conform to the letter of every legal and constitutional provision in the exercise of their powers, and yet remain fully subordinate to the legislative authority in all areas, is to expect nothing less than an ideal world—one in which the trustworthiness of chief executives never is at issue; the legal and constitutional provisions pertaining to the presidency are unmistakably clear and consistent, and do not unduly constrain the exercise of presidential authority; and legislators are concerned only with high-minded matters of policy and the public good. As the founders understood so well, such a state of affairs never will exist given the undeniable flaws of human beings. There are better ways to check the potential abuse of power than total elimination of the source of power. The dilemma of executive privilege can be resolved by means other than eliminating that authority altogether or effectively trying to do so through the use of onerous legalistic constraints.

Furthermore, the pro-imperial presidency view—the one in which the chief executive exercises his authority unfettered by congressional constraints, Congress defers to executive fiat, and the only check on presidential power takes place on election day—also misunderstands the separation of powers doctrine. The resolution to the dilemma of executive privilege is not simply to allow the president to determine for himself the scope and limits of his own authority.

Understanding the Separation of Powers

Only a proper understanding of the separation of powers doctrine can resolve the dilemma of executive privilege and the right to know. Such an understanding begins with the writings of the most influential thinkers of modern constitutionalism, [John] Locke and [Baron de] Montesquieu. Locke articulated a system of separated powers to limit the potential for governmental tyranny. As Louis W. Koenig has written, "John Locke would have been flabbergasted" by the Nixon assertion that any action undertaken by the president is legal. Yet limited governmental power can never bow to the "fundamental law of nature" that counsels self-preservation. Therefore, Locke advocated a strong executive, capable of acting with unity and "dispatch," and given the "power to act with discretion, for the public good, without the prescription of the law, and sometimes against it." Montesquieu similarly advocated a governmental system in which power checks power while still leaving the executive independent of direct popular will when necessary.

A proper understanding of the separation of powers also is rooted in the founding period and the early years of the Republic. The founders recognized an implied constitutional prerogative of presidential secrecy—a power that they believed was necessary and proper. The leading founders either exercised or acknowledged the right of executive branch secrecy in the early years of the Republic. In devising our constitutional system, they sought to limit governmental powers to reduce the threat of tyranny. But this perceived need to limit power never implied either weak government or a subordinate executive branch. As political scientist L. Peter Schultz has written, "The separation of powers constitutes an attempt to solve one of the major problems of government, that of providing for both reasonable government and forceful government without sacrificing either."

The leading founders exercised considerable foresight in establishing a constitutional system capable of adapting to the needs of changing times. That foresight has been especially useful to the conduct of foreign policy—the area in which claims of executive privilege are especially compelling. When it came to writing the executive articles of the Constitution, the Framers exercised great care not to constrain executive power with constitutional exactitude.

> There are inherent limitations on the prerogative powers of the presidency.

Finally, a proper understanding of the separation of powers doctrine is founded on the notion that there are inherent limitations on the prerogative powers of the presidency. The eventual resolution of the Nixon administration scandals shows that Congress and the judiciary, when given good reason to believe that the claim of privilege is being abused, have institutional mechanisms that can be used to compel the president to divulge information. The separation of powers system provides the vital mechanisms by which the other branches of government can challenge executive claims of privilege.

The answer to the question of how executive privilege can properly be exercised and constrained is found in an examination of the roles of the other branches of government in ensuring that the executive branch does not abuse the right to withhold information.

"Deep Throat" Was No Hero

George Putnam

The leading anonymous source for the *Washington Post*'s revelations about the Watergate scandal was far from the heroic figure some journalists have portrayed, asserts the following viewpoint. Instead, the man known as Deep Throat—who turned out to be Mark Felt of the FBI—was someone who leaked information in order to harm others. The writer of this viewpoint questions whether Felt's disclosure of President Nixon's acts was an action motivated by revenge. George Putnam was a long-serving news reporter and talk show host on both television and radio.

It is this reporter's opinion that, thirty years after Watergate, "Deep Throat" is finally revealed. Who would have thought that the Watergate source of the sordid story would originate with the then-second-top man at the FBI—a man named W. Mark Felt. Who would have thought that the trusted agent, having sworn

---

SOURCE. George Putnam, "One Reporter's Opinion—Is Felt a Hero or a Villain?," *Newsmax*, June 3, 2005. Reproduced by permission.

W. Mark Felt, former associate director of the FBI, and his wife, Audrey, appear on NBC's *Today* show in April 1978. Felt was later identified as "Deep Throat." (**AP Photo/Bob Daugherty.**)

an oath to country and the FBI, would scurry about back alleys at night passing out sensitive information to the detriment of his own government?

Is He a Hero or a Villain?

What was his motivation? Was it the fact that Nixon failed to name him J. Edgar Hoover's successor as top man at the FBI? It is a known fact that Felt held a grudge against Nixon because Nixon nominated then Assistant Attorney General Patrick Gray, and not Felt, to head the FBI.

Felt's "Deep Throat" revelation is not the only incident indicative of his character. In November 1980, Felt and Edward S. Miller, then head of the FBI Intelligence Division, were convicted of authorizing break-ins (without warrants) into the homes of family members of the Weather Underground, a radical antiwar group in the 1970s.

And so the story that Mark Felt was "Deep Throat" exposes old fissures, and those fissures are alive and can burst open because a wound this size—all this death, all this loss—doesn't really heal.

It was later revealed that Nixon actually testified on Felt's behalf. Yet Felt and his wife said they were betrayed by the country he had served and Felt blamed the trial for contributing to the death of his wife in 1984.

According to NewsMax.com Wires, White House insider Charles Colson, special counsel to President Nixon, tells of talking with Felt frequently and trusting him with very sensitive material, as did the president. He feels that Felt could have done the honorable thing (if he thought things were going wrong in the White House) by walking into FBI Director Pat Gray's office and putting a stop to Watergate.

Colson, who served seven months in prison for his part in the Watergate scandal, knew Richard Nixon intimately. Says Colson: "Nixon was no paragon of moral virtue. He would not necessarily have said: 'Oh my goodness, let me get to the bottom of this. It's terrible.' But he would have known that the director of the FBI and his deputy knew these things and he would call an end to this kind of stuff."

> 'Mark Felt could have stopped Watergate. . . . Instead, he [undermined] the administration.'

Colson reiterated: "Mark Felt could have stopped Watergate. He was in the position of that kind of influence. Instead, he goes out and basically undermines the administration. I don't think that's honorable at all."

It is this reporter's opinion that Felt is not a hero. But what will Felt's fate be? Will Felt be used as he has used others? Many believe Felt's real motivation in revealing himself as "Deep Throat" is MONEY—that Felt's daughter urged him to tell all so that the inevitable resulting profits would send her kids to college.

Felt is a pathetic individual who, having suffered a stroke, is now in failing health and is, at 91 years of age, to be pitied. But the fact remains: Felt chose to be a scoundrel rather than a genuine American hero. His fate is of his own making.

Henry Kissinger views Felt as "a troubled man." But he adds, "I have always believed and continue to believe that there was not one 'Deep Throat.'"

Anonymous Sources Must Have Their Secrecy Protected

Zachary Coile

The revelation of the true identity of Watergate's "Deep Throat" provided an occasion to note that anonymous sources were a necessity in uncovering Watergate illegalities as well as government wrongdoing since then, Zachary Coile reports in the following article. Coile quotes a range of media experts who assert that certain information crucial to the public can be obtained only by granting anonymity. This is true even though the practice risks the credibility of journalism—as a few scandals at prominent newspapers have demonstrated. The prevailing media view is that anonymity should be granted as infrequently as possible but still employed when necessary. After a career as a political reporter for the *San Francisco Chronicle*, in 2009 Zachary Coile joined the staff of US senator Barbara Boxer of California.

Anonymous sources have been condemned by the [George W.] Bush White House as a threat to the credibility of the media and called an "evil of journalism" by *USA Today* founder Al Neuharth.

But even as news organizations scramble to write new policies to limit their reliance on unnamed sources, the unveiling Tuesday [May 31, 2005] of the world's most famous anonymous source, Deep Throat, reminds the media and the public why their use is sometimes necessary, journalism experts say.

The *Washington Post* confirmed Tuesday that 91-year-old W. Mark Felt, the FBI's No. 2 official during the early 1970s who now lives in Santa Rosa, was the secret source for stories by reporters Bob Woodward and Carl Bernstein that helped bring down Richard Nixon's presidency in the Watergate scandal.

"It is deeply ironic that the mother of all anonymous sources—which precipitated some really tectonic changes in the American political scene, including the resignation of a president—should be coming forward at a time when anonymous sources are being so impugned," said Orville Schell, dean of the Graduate School of Journalism at UC Berkeley. "I think it would be an incalculable loss to this country if all anonymous sources became forbidden, particularly in this era of governmental and corporate secrecy—and I might add, ecclesiastical secrecy. The price has been raised very high for whistle-blowers."

The use of unnamed sources has been under fire recently after *Newsweek* retracted a story last month that cited anonymous sources claiming that investigators at Guantanamo Bay prison in Cuba believed U.S. guards flushed a Quran down the toilet to unnerve Muslim prisoners.

Newsweek apologized for the story, which some cite as the reason for deadly riots that followed in Afghanistan, saying the unnamed source of the report had backed away from his initial claims after the story was published.

An Amnesty International report last week found that a prisoner at Guantanamo Bay had complained that a Quran was flushed in a toilet, but a Pentagon inquiry found no evidence to back up the claim.

The *Newsweek* controversy led White House spokesman Scott McClellan to complain about "a credibility problem in the media regarding the use of anonymous sources."

Reporting the Truth Can Be Risky

But media experts said that while news organizations take a risk in relying on unnamed sources, it is often the only way to uncover some information.

Afghan college students burn a US flag during a protest against the alleged desecration of the Koran by US troops at the Guantanamo Bay detention center that was reported by *Newsweek* citing anonymous sources but later retracted. (Shah Marai/AFP/Getty Images.)

"There are certain kinds of reporting that cannot be done without sources who are unnamed, in particular reporting on national security or defense . . . because people jeopardize their careers and in some cases their legal status by disclosing things," said James Bettinger, a longtime reporter and editor at the *Riverside Press-Enterprise* and the *San Jose Mercury News* who directs the John S. Knight journalism fellowship program at Stanford University.

"That said, there is too great a reliance on anonymous sources," Bettinger said. "That's why every news organization I know of is trying to reduce their use or their reliance on anonymous sources."

> 'Deep Throat represents the kind of source that a lot of reporters would like to have.'

Woodward and Bernstein issued a statement Tuesday saying Felt "helped us immeasurably in our Watergate coverage," although they said many other sources were also involved. Former *Washington Post* Editor Ben Bradlee told the paper: "The No. 2 guy at the FBI—that was a pretty good source."

"Deep Throat represents the kind of source that a lot of reporters would like to have," Bettinger said. "He served as someone that Woodward could go to on a regular basis and say, 'Are we on the right track?' . . . That is a huge fear of every good reporter, 'Do we have this right?'"

Many papers began re-examining their policies on the use of unnamed sources in 2003 after the *New York Times* acknowledged it had failed to adequately check sources quoted by reporter Jayson Blair, who was fired for fabricating stories.

The Blair scandal and the forced resignation of *USA Today* reporter Jack Kelley for similar charges prompted Neuharth to write a Jan. 15, 2004, column calling for a media wide ban on anonymous sources. "Until or unless we do, the public won't trust us, and we put the First Amendment in jeopardy," he wrote.

But some journalists have recently spoken out about the need for anonymous sources. Daniel Schorr, senior news analyst for NPR radio, wrote in a syndicated column last week that unnamed sources provided the first photos and accounts of abuse at Abu Ghraib prison in Iraq, as well as a 2,000-page secret file of an Army investigation about the torture and killing of two prisoners in Afghanistan, recently reported by the *New York Times*.

"On many vital matters, we would be left in the dark were it not for leaks," Schorr wrote.

Brooks Jackson, a longtime reporter for the Associated Press, the *Wall Street Journal* and CNN, said the mistake often made—as seen in the *Newsweek* case—is to rely on an unnamed source who is a step removed from the news.

"Often it's second-hand information, and if that's not made clear, then the reader is not being served very well," said Jackson, who now directs www.factcheck.org, a nonpartisan group.

Pardoning Nixon Benefited the Country

Evan Thomas

In the following viewpoint, the former editor at large of *Newsweek* discusses President Gerald Ford's pardon of former president Richard Nixon in dealing with the Watergate scandal. The author covers the events leading up to the presidential pardon and the public backlash afterward. He contends history shows that Ford made the right decision. Evan Thomas is the author of eight books and more than one hundred cover articles. He teaches journalism at Princeton University.

On the morning of Sunday, Sept. 8, 1974, after he had been president for about a month, Gerald Ford took communion at St. John's Episcopal Church on Lafayette Square, across from the White House. He prayed alone in the presidential pew. On the way out the church door, he sloughed off report-

SOURCE. Evan Thomas, "The 38th President: More than Met the Eye," *Newsweek*, January 7, 2007. Copyright © 2007 by Newsweek. All rights reserved. Reproduced by permission.

ers who were badgering him about his plans for the day—"You'll find out soon enough," he said. Back in the Oval Office, he telephoned Sen. Barry Goldwater, the fabled conservative, to tell him he was pardoning Richard Nixon for whatever crimes the disgraced president might have committed in office. Goldwater, whose voice had been critical in forcing Nixon's resignation, was dumbfounded. "It doesn't make any sense," he protested. Ford answered, "The public has the right to know that, in the eyes of the president, Nixon is clear." Goldwater responded: "He may be clear in your eyes, but he's not clear in mine."

Next, Ford called his old congressional adversary, the then House Majority Leader Thomas P. (Tip) O'Neill, and told him that he intended to pardon Nixon. "I'm telling you right now," O'Neill said, "this will cost you the election. I hope it's not part of any deal."

"No," Ford replied calmly, "there's no deal."

"Then why the hell are you doing it?" O'Neill asked.

Ford answered that Nixon was a "sick man" and that his daughter Julie "keeps calling me because her father is so depressed." O'Neill was unpersuaded, but Ford seemed determined. A few minutes later that Sunday morning, the president went on national television to announce his decision. Ford's own aides had been dubious about the pardon and had tried to argue with him. But Ford moved—quickly, at first secretly, then decisively—to cut off any criminal prosecution of his predecessor. Ford had experienced no trouble sleeping the night before—"Once I determine to move, I seldom, if ever, fret," he recalled in his memoirs. After announcing the pardon, Ford recorded, he felt "an unbelievable lifting of a burden from my shoulders." He went off to play golf.

> Conventional wisdom has shifted: pardoning Nixon . . . spared the nation an ordeal of recrimination and allowed the healing to begin.

White House chief of staff Alexander Haig has been accused of arranging Richard Nixon's pardon by Gerald Ford. **(David Hume Kennerly/Gerald R. Ford Presidential Library/ Getty Images.)**

Public Backlash

O'Neill's warning was not wrong. The public hammering Ford took for pardoning Nixon probably *did* cost him the election in 1976. "Jail Ford!" screamed angry crowds, who widely assumed (not altogether without reason) that Nixon had wrangled a deal. Most newspapers in the righteous post-Watergate era gravely editorialized against Ford's action. His own press secretary, Jerry terHorst, quit in disgust.

Yet, more than three decades later, Ford's decision has been largely vindicated. The conventional wisdom has shifted: pardoning Nixon was the farsighted thing to do. It spared the nation an ordeal of recrimination and allowed the healing to begin. . . .

Ford was a close ally and admirer of Nixon's from their days together in the House Chowder and Marching Society, a band of hard-charging GOP congressmen who voted, logrolled and played together. As the GOP House leader after Nixon's election in 1968, Ford faithfully did the bidding of Nixon's attorney general, John Mitchell, by leading a clumsy attempt to impeach Supreme Court Justice William O. Douglas. Ford attacked Douglas as "senile" and for allowing his writings to be published in a "pornographic magazine" called Avant Garde. The impeachment effort collapsed after a couple of weeks; Ford later admitted the whole thing had been a "mistake."

When the first flames of Watergate began to singe the White House, Ford remained loyal. At Nixon's urging, Ford was instrumental in making sure that the House Banking and Currency Committee did not investigate the source of freshly printed $100 bills that turned up on the Watergate burglars. He was rewarded when Vice President Spiro Agnew pleaded no contest to accepting payoffs and was forced to resign in October 1973. Recognizing that Ford was the safest bet for congressional confirmation, Nixon chose him to replace Agnew.

As the Watergate scandal deepened, Ford had to walk a fine line between supporting the president and not going down with him. He was careful never to ask Nixon if he was guilty of covering up the Watergate break-in. But the vice president's suspicions were growing. His way of dealing with them in the spring of 1974 was to get out of town. "He deliberately fled Washington, very deliberately," recalls Ford's former House speechwriter and close aide Bob Hartmann. "He just told me to accept every invitation he possibly could. His travel itinerary was nearly continuous. He was not being devious. On the other hand, he was nobody's fool." In his public appearances, Ford began to "zig-zag—to be intentionally inconsistent in his comments," writes former Ford adviser James Cannon. "One day the tilt would be favorable: Nixon is innocent of an impeachable offense, he would say. The next day he would tilt against him."

Ford's deft balancing act during Nixon's fall drew little attention as investigators and reporters stalked bigger game. Sympathetic White House aides protected Ford by distancing him from the scandals, deleting his remarks from the edited transcripts of meetings or marking them "unintelligible." But Ford and Nixon were heading toward a high-stakes drama that is one of the most intriguing—and still somewhat murky—acts in the whole Shakespearean tragedy.

Without ever explicitly acknowledging what they were doing, Ford and Nixon began a private dance concerning the delicate question of whether Ford might pardon Nixon if the president stepped down and Ford took his place. Neither man could be seen participating in such a crude transaction. That does not mean, however, that there weren't some clever machinations and manipulations—on both sides.

The go-between in this shadow play was former Army general Alexander Haig, Nixon's chief of staff. Haig had been acting as a kind of regent, running the government while Nixon withdrew to the White House residence to brood while listening to "Victory at Sea" before roaring fires. At once scheming, dutiful and imperious, Haig was trying to protect the president—but, at the same time, get Nixon out of office before the president could be impeached in the House and convicted by the Senate. And if Nixon could be persuaded to resign, Haig wanted to insulate him from being prosecuted in the courts. Hence the call Ford received shortly after 8 on the morning of Aug. 1, 1974.

Haig wanted to know if he could come to Ford's office at the Old Executive Office Building. "It's urgent," said Haig. "I want to alert you that things are deteriorating. The whole ball game may be over. You'd better start thinking about a change in your life." That was not all Haig wanted to tell Ford. But according to Ford's memoirs, "A Time to Heal," Haig seemed reluctant to talk in front of Bob Hartmann, who was also in the room.

Haig decided to come back in the afternoon. This time he caught Ford alone in his office. Haig explained that the White House was turning over a tape recording—later known as the "smoking gun" tape—to the courts. On the tape, Nixon could be heard obstructing justice by trying to get the CIA to head off an FBI investigation of the Watergate break-in. Haig began to lay out various options before he got to the ones that mattered. He had brought two pieces of paper with him. Nixon's chief of staff explained to Ford that the president could resign and be pardoned by his successor. One piece of paper summarized a president's authority to grant such a pardon; the other was an actual pardon form.

"Al," Ford said, "I need some time to think about this." As Haig left, Ford sat back, he later recalled, and thought to himself, "I am about to become president. It's going to happen."

> Nixon's chief of staff explained to Ford that the president could resign and be pardoned by his successor.

Hartmann came into the veep's [vice-president's] office, and Ford told him that Nixon would resign if Ford would pardon him. Hartmann burst out, "Jesus! What did you tell him?" "I didn't tell him anything," Ford responded. "I told him I needed time to think about it." "You what?" Hartmann asked. "That's almost the worst answer Haig could take back to the White House. You told Haig you are willing to entertain the idea of a pardon if he resigns—that's probably all Haig and Nixon want to know."

Ford told Hartmann that he was overreacting. That night, as he lay in bed with [his wife] Betty, Ford pondered what to do. In his memoirs, he wrote that Haig called him at 1 A.M. to tell him that "nothing had changed" and that the situation "remained fluid." Ford recalled that he told Haig, "I've talked with Betty, and we're prepared, but we can't get involved in the White House decision making process." But according to Barry Werth's "31 Days," the most authoritative retelling of Ford's roller-coaster first month in office, Ford told a different story to his aides the next morning. According to Hartmann, Ford told him: "Betty and I talked it over last night . . . We felt we were ready. This just has to stop; it's tearing the country to pieces. I decided to go ahead and get it over with, so I called Al Haig and told them they should do whatever they decided to do, it was all right with me." Aghast that Haig and Nixon might interpret Ford's words as a signal that a pardon would follow a resignation, his aides—including Hartmann, John Marsh and Bryce Harlow—implored the vice president to call Haig right away. Ford should tell the president's chief of staff, unambiguously, that nothing they had discussed should be construed as a deal. Ford agreed and made the call, reading from notecards.

> The fact that he did agree to pardon Nixon . . . , Ford always insisted, was unrelated to his discussions with Haig before Nixon resigned.

In later years, Haig would deny that he had offered Ford any kind of deal, denials he publicly repeated last week. Ford, for his part, professed a kind of wounded innocence. In 1997 he told *Washington Post* reporter Bob Woodward: "Well, I guess I was naive. I was naive that anybody would offer a deal because all my political life people never came to me, 'I'm going to give you a political donation. I expect something in return.' People never came to me that way, because they knew damn well I wouldn't be part of it." In any case, "it never became a deal because I never accepted," said Ford. The fact that he did agree to pardon Nixon 31 days after assuming the presidency, Ford always insisted, was unrelated to his discussions with Haig before Nixon resigned. . . .

The Nixon pardon did go a long way to ensure "domestic tranquility" in the American family.

Why Pardoning Nixon Was Wrong

Timothy Noah

As the years went by, more than a few prominent opponents of Richard Nixon's pardon changed their public positions, but a basic fact remains: It is never right to pardon someone before establishing what the person is being pardoned for, argues the author of the following viewpoint. The rationales that Gerald Ford offered for the pardon—including that he was concerned about Nixon's health—do not stand up to scrutiny, he says. Even if Nixon had happened to be in grave condition, justice would not have been served by a hasty pardon, he asserts, and in fact Nixon went on to live another active twenty years. Timothy Noah has written for publications including *Slate, Washington Monthly, U.S. News & World Report, Newsweek, New Republic,* and the *Wall Street Journal.*

I n the days since Gerald Ford's death, so much praise has been heaped on the late president's blanket pardon to his predecessor, Richard Nixon, that you'd

---

SOURCE. Timothy Noah, "Why Pardoning Nixon Was Wrong," *Slate,* December 29, 2006. Reproduced by permission.

think Tricky Dick was Jean Valjean. These magnanimous pronouncements are a preening exercise in cost-free generosity three decades after the fact. They reflect little or no consideration of the merits of the pardon itself.

No new information has emerged during the past 32 years that makes Ford's pardon to Nixon look any more justifiable; indeed, what facts have dribbled forth make it seem less so. (More on these later.) Nor can the pardon plausibly be considered an example of the bipartisan spirit for which Ford is justly, if too extravagantly, praised by Washington insiders. The pardon may have had the long-term *effect* of tamping down partisan warfare between Democrats and Republicans over a possible criminal trial (obstruction of justice would have been the likeliest charge), but when a Republican short-circuits prosecution of a fellow Republican, you can't call that bipartisanship. These logical obstacles help explain why people who defend the pardon today do so with vague language about how, in retrospect, it was better for the country to set rancor aside and move on. Roger Wilkins, who as an editorial writer for the *New York Times* condemned the pardon back in 1974, wrote Ford last month to tell him he has since changed his mind. (The *Times* itself, wisely, has not.) Here's what Wilkins told the *Washington Post*:

> When a Republican short-circuits prosecution of a fellow Republican, you can't call that bipartisanship.

> Ford was right. The country really needed to move on. The picture of a president in the dock with these motley Democrats hounding him, it would have made the country—we'd gone through some ugly times, but it would have been uglier. . . . If Ford hadn't done a thing else in his presidency, that would have been a great service to the country.

Sen. Edward Kennedy, D-Mass., is another person who denounced the pardon in 1974 but subsequently changed his mind:

> Unlike many of us at the time, President Ford recognized that the nation had to move forward, and could not do so if there was a continuing effort to prosecute former President Nixon. His courage and dedication to our country made it possible for us to begin the process of healing and put the tragedy of Watergate behind us.

Kennedy uttered these words at a 2001 ceremony at the John F. Kennedy Library and Museum in which Ford was presented with a Profile in Courage award, named for JFK's famous book about U.S. senators who risked all to do what is right. The committee that chose Ford included David McCullough, John Seigenthaler, Marian Wright Edelman, and Elaine Jones; I'd be surprised if a single one of them thought the pardon was a good idea back in 1974. At the Kennedy Library, Ford shared the podium with Rep. John Lewis, D-Ga., who was also given a Profile in Courage award that year. The magnitude of their respective sacrifices were, to say the least, divergent. Lewis suffered more than 40 beatings and arrests in order to bring basic rights to African-Americans. Ford suffered an early and extremely lucrative retirement (golfing and sitting on eight corporate boards) in order to keep Richard Nixon out of jail.

Why was Ford wrong to pardon Nixon? Mainly because it set a bad precedent. Nixon had not yet been indicted, let alone convicted, of any crime. It's never a good idea to pardon somebody without at least finding out first what you're pardoning him *for*. How can you possibly weigh the quality of mercy against considerations of justice? Yet it would happen again in December 1992, when departing President George H.W. Bush pardoned Caspar Weinberger, former defense secretary, 12 days before Weinberger was set to go to trial for perjury.

As I've noted before, this was almost certainly done to prevent evidence concerning Bush's own involvement in Iran-contra (when he was vice-president) from becoming public. The final report from Iran-contra special prosecutor Lawrence Walsh called it "the first time a President ever pardoned someone in whose trial he might have been called as a witness," but in fact it was the second. Ford's motive was less self-protective, but, as *Slate*'s Christopher Hitchens notes, it had the same effect of shutting down further investigation into illegal activities. Without the precedent of Ford's pre-emptive pardon, Bush *père* might have lacked the nerve to attempt one

Protestors opposed to President Ford's pardon of Richard Nixon gather on September 9, 1974. **(Bill Pierce/Time & Life Pictures/Getty Images.)**

> "Odds are that no prosecution would have taken place."

himself, and certainly would have created a much bigger ruckus if he went ahead and did it anyway.

If Ford *hadn't* issued the pardon, would Nixon have stood trial, or perhaps even been sent to jail? If so, his successors might have learned the valuable lesson that presidents are not above the law. But odds are that no prosecution would have taken place. In a Dec. 28 editorial, the *Wall Street Journal* stated that Watergate Special Prosecutor Leon Jaworski "seemed determined to pursue" a criminal trial. The precise opposite is true. By his own account, Jaworski was reluctant to pursue prosecutorial alternatives to impeachment. James Cannon's 1994 book *Time and Chance: Gerald Ford's Appointment With History* quotes Jaworski saying, "I knew in my own mind that if an indictment were returned and the court asked me if I believed Nixon could receive a prompt, fair trial as guaranteed by the Constitution, I would have replied in the negative." In a Dec. 29 op-ed in the *Washington Post*, Jaworski's former employee, Richard Ben-Veniste—yet *another* person who changed his mind and now thinks Ford was right to pardon Nixon—writes that Jaworski was "of the view that Nixon's precipitous fall from the highest office was punishment enough." Even if Jaworski had been talked into indicting Nixon, the prosecution's constitutionality—at best, uncertain—would have been a matter for the courts to decide, and the judiciary tends to err on the side of caution when considering separation of powers. That probably helps explain why President Bill Clinton was never indicted for perjury, even after congressional efforts to remove him from office failed.

Bob Woodward (another member of the "I can't believe I'm a Nixon defender" club) wrote extensively about the Ford pardon in his 1999 book *Shadow: Five Presidents and the Legacy of Watergate*, and after Ford's death,

The Treatment of Watergate at the Nixon Library

The establishment of an official presidential library to preserve the legacy of each president after leaving office began in 1939, but no presidential library has faced such a dilemma as Richard Nixon's. Much happened during his two terms, but what should this official archive show about the only president to resign in disgrace?

The solution, after decades of controversy, was to construct a Watergate Gallery within the Richard Nixon Presidential Library and Museum. It is the complex's largest gallery.

In an April 1, 2011, article, the *New York Times* said the gallery "offers a searing and often unforgiving account of one of the most painful chapters of the nation's history." It even allows visitors to listen to some of the secret Nixon recordings.

The gallery did not open until 2011, almost forty years after Nixon's resignation. Designed and organized by professional historians, the gallery replaced an exhibition that had been created by the Nixon Foundation, a group of Nixon supporters. That group's depiction of Watergate was as "an orchestrated effort by Democrats to overturn the 1972 election," the *Times* reported.

The Nixon Presidential Library and Museum is located in Yorba Linda, California, Nixon's birthplace.

he recycled that reporting in the *Washington Post*. The gist of Woodward's account is that immediately prior to Nixon's resignation, Nixon's chief of staff, Alexander Haig, offered what Ford interpreted to be a *quid pro quo*: Nixon will leave if you guarantee him a pardon. (Haig denies that he proposed one in exchange for the other.) Ford answered that he would have to think about it. After an aide pointed out to him that such a deal would be outrageously improper, Ford phoned Haig to say, "No deal." But the very next day, Ford told another aide that he would pardon Nixon: A month later, President Ford did so. We can argue about whether this sequence of events constituted an implicit deal, but at the very least, we must conclude that the pardon was Nixon's idea, not Ford's.

Woodward further reports that when Ford issued the pardon, he was very concerned about the state of Nixon's health. Nixon and Ford, Woodward reported in a Dec. 29 *Washington Post* piece (the *Post* has given Ford's death the kind of extensive coverage usually reserved for the start of a major war), were much better friends than people ever realized. These details lend a human perspective to Ford's decision to pardon Nixon, and spotlight Ford's undeniable decency. But pardons aren't supposed to be granted on the basis of friendship. As for Nixon's health, I don't recall many tears being shed this past July when Kenneth Lay, then awaiting sentencing after his conspiracy and fraud convictions, breathed his last. Can anyone doubt that Lay's prosecution probably contributed to his death? Would anyone argue that Lay therefore should never have been prosecuted? (In the event, Nixon lived 20 years more after his resignation, remaining active to the last and dying at 81.)

> " Nixon's pardon . . . did not serve the interests of justice. "

I don't mean to overstate my opposition to Nixon's pardon. I didn't think it was a world-shattering calamity then, and I don't think it was a world-shattering calamity now. But it did not serve the interests of justice, it had an unfortunate consequence in the Weinberger pardon, and it carried a mild whiff of corruption. Ford placed great stock in the fact that, according to a 1915 Supreme Court decision in *Burdick v. United States*, acceptance of a pardon constitutes an admission of guilt. But in May 1977, Nixon the ex-president would tell David Frost, "When the president does it, that means that it is not illegal." Which do you remember—that quotation, or *Burdick v. United States*, a copy of which Ford would carry around with him for the rest of his life? Pardoning Nixon was wrong, and the death of the very nice man who did it does not change that.

The Lessons of Watergate Should Never Disappear

Elizabeth Drew

Watergate was indicative of the attitude President Richard Nixon's administration demonstrated right from the start, declares the author of the following viewpoint. People who disagreed with the president were labeled as enemies—essentially, criminals—and the administration used government resources against them. If Nixon's abuses of power had not been revealed and stopped, the United States was headed for fascism, the author asserts. Those who say that Nixon could never have gotten away with it and that the system worked are ignoring how close a call it was at the time. What happened throughout that era instructs Americans on how and why to protect the Constitution, she says. Elizabeth Drew was the Washington correspondent for the *Atlantic* and *New Yorker* magazines from 1967 to 1992 and has written eleven books about politicians and government, including the biography *Richard M. Nixon.*

SOURCE. Elizabeth Drew, "Why Watergate Matters," *Los Angeles Times,* June 17, 2007. Copyright © 2007 by Elizabeth Drew. All rights reserved. Reproduced by permission.

Today [June 2007] marks the 35th anniversary of one of the most famous and most misunderstood events in modern American history: the break-in at the Democratic National Committee's [DNC] headquarters in the Watergate office building on June 17, 1972. The break-in set off a chain of events known as "Watergate," which led ultimately to Richard Nixon's forced resignation as president—and which is also misunderstood. For history's sake, it's important to set these things straight.

The break-in became famous, of course, because the inept burglars got caught by the night watchman—did they not expect that there would be one?—who called the police, who in turn called in the FBI and federal prosecutors. But it was in fact the fourth attempt by the burglars and their supervisors, E. Howard Hunt and G. Gordon Liddy—collectively known as the "plumbers"— to get into the DNC offices and, among other things, place a tap on the telephone of the party chairman, Lawrence O'Brien.

The plumbers got their label because they had originally been hired by the Nixon White House to plug leaks to the press; Nixon had been particularly enraged by Daniel Ellsberg's 1971 leak of the Pentagon Papers, a study of the [Lyndon] Johnson administration's conduct of the Vietnam War. (Nixon feared that the study would reflect badly on his own handling of the war, and besides, he hated leaks.)

> " The plumbers were almost comically inept. . . . But their bungling did not make what they were about any less sinister. "

The first attempted break-in failed because the conspirators got locked in a closet off the main dining room of the Watergate complex. The next one didn't work because the burglars—most of them Cubans and veterans of President [John F.] Kennedy's failed invasion of the Bay of Pigs—couldn't figure out how to pick the lock on

In 2002, the US National Archives displayed some of the police evidence from the Watergate break-in that had been warehoused for almost thirty years. In the background are arrest photo enlargements of the men who broke into the Democratic Party offices. (Paul J. Richards/ AFP/Getty Images.)

the committee's door. After that, one of the burglars returned home to Miami to collect better equipment.

During the Memorial Day weekend of 1972, the burglars first succeeded in entering the party headquarters, where they photographed documents and placed taps on the phones of O'Brien and another committee aide. But the tap on O'Brien's phone wasn't placed correctly, and John Mitchell, the former attorney general who was head of Nixon's reelection committee, told Liddy to go back and fix the tap. Liddy readily agreed; by this time, it was no big deal.

The plumbers were almost comically inept in this and other operations, including a raid the previous year on the Beverly Hills office of Dr. Lewis Fielding, Ellsberg's psychiatrist. They had broken in to seize the file on Ellsberg, but when they got there, they found no files at all.

But their bungling did not make what they were about any less sinister.

Watergate Was a Constitutional Crisis

Watergate was not merely an event, or even a series of events, but a mentality that permeated Nixon's presidency from the beginning. Within a month after he was sworn in in 1969, Nixon instructed his aides to set up a secret office, paid for by private (and therefore illegal) funds, to "get the goods," as he put it, on his perceived enemies. The first assignment for these White House-hired gumshoes was to tail Sen. Edward M. Kennedy of Massachusetts, who Nixon thought might be his Democratic opponent for reelection.

> The Nixon operation was like a step on the road to fascism.

Think of it: an American president considering political opponents and other domestic critics—hardly people armed with nuclear weapons—his "enemies." And then using the instruments of government, such as the Internal Revenue Service, against them. ("Crush them" was another oft-used Nixon phrase.) Nothing like this is known to have happened at any other time in U.S. history.

The break-in at the DNC and other actions (such as the hiring of Donald Segretti to disrupt and create chaos at Democratic Party events) portray a president intent on undermining and even interfering with the opposition party's nominating process. In that sense, the Nixon operation was like a step on the road to fascism. The first thing a usurper does is undermine the opposition party.

Watergate was not, as some Nixon defenders still argue heatedly, a "mere" burglary and cover-up. It was a

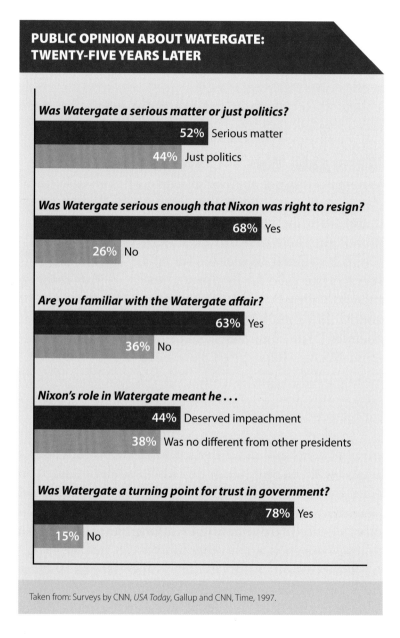

PUBLIC OPINION ABOUT WATERGATE: TWENTY-FIVE YEARS LATER

Was Watergate a serious matter or just politics?

52% Serious matter

44% Just politics

Was Watergate serious enough that Nixon was right to resign?

68% Yes

26% No

Are you familiar with the Watergate affair?

63% Yes

36% No

Nixon's role in Watergate meant he...

44% Deserved impeachment

38% Was no different from other presidents

Was Watergate a turning point for trust in government?

78% Yes

15% No

Taken from: Surveys by CNN, *USA Today*, Gallup and CNN, Time, 1997.

constitutional crisis. The raid on Ellsberg's psychiatrist's office was a clear violation of the Fourth Amendment's prohibition against unwarranted searches and seizures. And Nixon was engaged in a systematic attempt to defy the courts and Congress—denying them information and seeking to make the executive branch unaccountable to the other branches of government.

At stake was whether our system of government would successfully withstand Nixon's abuse of power. It's become a settled part of history that "the system worked." But it almost didn't. Many members of Congress were loath to move against Nixon until they found a "smoking gun"—in a roomful of smoke.

But even before the smoking gun was found—a tape on which Nixon instructed his top aide, H.R. (Bob) Haldeman, to tell the CIA to tell the FBI to drop the Watergate case, on the (nonexistent) ground of a threat to national security—the House Judiciary Committee had decided on bipartisan votes that Nixon had committed impeachable offenses.

The committee's deliberations were serious and careful. This was no partisan lynch mob out to "get" Nixon; his fate was sealed not by the "liberal media," as Nixon die-hards said and still say, but by a thoughtful group of members of Congress of both parties, as well as the office of the independent counsel, which Nixon had been forced to appoint. In the end, it was a small group of Republican congressional leaders who went to the White House and told Nixon that he had to resign.

All of this matters not only because it's an important part of American history but because it is a cautionary tale about overreaching for power, abuse of the office of the presidency, and about protecting the Constitution. Such things matter a lot.

CHAPTER 3

Personal Narratives

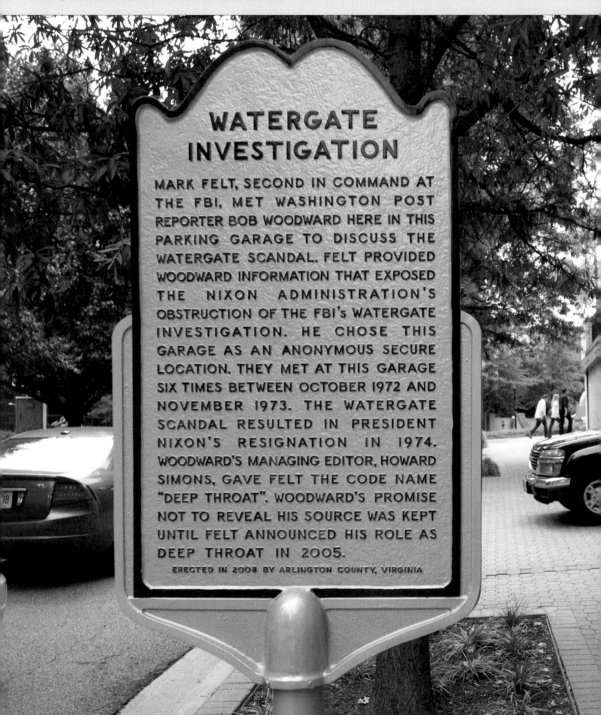

WATERGATE INVESTIGATION

MARK FELT, SECOND IN COMMAND AT THE FBI, MET WASHINGTON POST REPORTER BOB WOODWARD HERE IN THIS PARKING GARAGE TO DISCUSS THE WATERGATE SCANDAL. FELT PROVIDED WOODWARD INFORMATION THAT EXPOSED THE NIXON ADMINISTRATION'S OBSTRUCTION OF THE FBI's WATERGATE INVESTIGATION. HE CHOSE THIS GARAGE AS AN ANONYMOUS SECURE LOCATION. THEY MET AT THIS GARAGE SIX TIMES BETWEEN OCTOBER 1972 AND NOVEMBER 1973. THE WATERGATE SCANDAL RESULTED IN PRESIDENT NIXON'S RESIGNATION IN 1974. WOODWARD'S MANAGING EDITOR, HOWARD SIMONS, GAVE FELT THE CODE NAME "DEEP THROAT". WOODWARD'S PROMISE NOT TO REVEAL HIS SOURCE WAS KEPT UNTIL FELT ANNOUNCED HIS ROLE AS DEEP THROAT IN 2005.

ERECTED IN 2008 BY ARLINGTON COUNTY, VIRGINIA

Watergate Should Have Been a "Little Thing"

Richard M. Nixon, interviewed by David Frost

In 1977, in his first major public appearance since resigning three years earlier, Richard Nixon responded to questions about Watergate in a televised interview with David Frost. At that time, Nixon maintained that the president has authority beyond the law, that the United Stated has essentially been at war during the time of Watergate, and that he did not endorse the break-in at the Democratic National Committee headquarters. He acknowledged being overly loyal to his top aides, but insisted the extent of his guilt was that he made a few mistakes regarding small matters. He did not commit crimes worth being impeached for, he asserted, yet he in effect impeached himself by resigning. The following is the transcript of the landmark interview. David Frost is a British journalist and has been a media personality since the early 1960s. Richard M. Nixon was the thirty-seventh president of the United States.

Photo on previous page: A marker notes the parking garage where reporter Bob Woodward met with his secret source. His reporting helped uncover the Watergate scandal. (**Saul Loeb**/ AFP/Getty Images.)

SOURCE. Richard Nixon, interviewed by David Frost, "I Have Impeached Myself," *The Guardian*, September 7, 2007. Copyright © 2007 by Sir David Frost. All rights reserved. Reproduced by permission.

*D*avid Frost: *The wave of dissent in America, occasionally violent, which followed the incursion into Cambodia by US and Vietnamese forces in 1970, prompted President Nixon to demand better intelligence about the people who were opposing him on the domestic front.*

To this end, the deputy White House counsel, Tom Huston, arranged a series of meetings with representatives of the CIA, the FBI, and other police and intelligence agencies.

These meetings produced a plan, the Huston Plan, which advocated the systematic use of wiretappings, burglaries, or so-called black bag jobs, mail openings and infiltration against anti-war groups and others. Some of these activities, as Huston emphasised to Nixon, were clearly illegal. Nevertheless, the president approved the plan. Five days later, after opposition from the FBI director, J Edgar Hoover, the plan was withdrawn, but the president's approval was later to be listed in the articles of impeachment as an alleged abuse of presidential power.

> When the president does it, that means it is not illegal.

Would you say that there are certain situations—and the Huston Plan was one of them—where the president can decide that it's in the best interests of the nation, and do something illegal?

Richard Nixon: Well, when the president does it, that means it is not illegal.

By definition.

Exactly, exactly. If the president, for example, approves something because of the national security, or in this case because of a threat to internal peace and order of significant magnitude, then the president's decision in that instance is one that enables those who carry it out, to carry it out without violating a law. Otherwise they're in an impossible position.

The point is: the dividing line is the president's judgment?

Yes, and, so that one does not get the impression that a president can run amok in this country and get away with it, we have to have in mind that a president has to come up before the electorate. We also have to have in mind that a president has to get appropriations from the Congress. We have to have in mind, for example, that as far as the CIA's covert operations are concerned, as far as the FBI's covert operations are concerned, through the years, they have been disclosed on a very, very limited basis to trusted members of Congress.

Speaking of the presidency, you stated: "It's quite obvious that there are certain inherently government activities, which, if undertaken by the sovereign in protection of the interests of the nation's security, are lawful, but which if undertaken by private persons, are not." What, at root, did you have in mind there?

Well, what I had in mind I think was perhaps much better stated by [Abraham] Lincoln during the war between the States. Lincoln said, and I think I can remember the quote almost exactly: "Actions which otherwise would be unconstitutional, could become lawful if undertaken for the purpose of preserving the constitution and the nation."

Now that's the kind of action I'm referring to. Of course in Lincoln's case it was the survival of the Union in wartime, it's the defense of the nation and, who knows, perhaps the survival of the nation.

But there is no comparison, is there, between the situation you faced and the situation Lincoln faced?

This nation was torn apart in an ideological way by the war in Vietnam, as much as the Civil War tore apart the nation when Lincoln was president. Now it's true that we didn't have the North and the South. . . .

But when you said, as you said when we were talking about the Huston Plan, "If the president orders it, that makes it legal," is there anything in the constitution or the bill of rights that suggests the president is that much of a sovereign, that far above the law?

No, there isn't. There's nothing specific that the constitution contemplates. I haven't read every word, every jot and every tittle, but I do know that it has been argued that, as far as a president is concerned, that in wartime, a president does have certain extraordinary powers which would make acts that would otherwise be unlawful, lawful if undertaken for the purpose of preserving the nation and the constitution, which is essential for the rights we're all talking about.

Watergate Recordings Indicate a Payoff

My reading of the transcript of the tapes tells me, trying to read them in an open-minded way, that the writing, not just between the lines, but on so many of the lines, is very, very clear—that you were, in fact, endorsing at least the short-term solution of paying this sum of money to buy time. That would be my reading of it. But the other point to be said is: here's [John] Dean [White House Counsel] talking about this hush money, for [one of the Watergate burglars, E Howard] Hunt, talking about blackmail and all of that. I would say that you endorsed or ratified it. But let's leave that on one side . . .

I didn't endorse or ratify it.

Why didn't you stop it?

Because at that point I had no knowledge of the fact that it was going to be paid.

What I don't understand about March 21 [1973, the date of the conversation with Dean] is that I still don't know why you didn't pick up the phone and tell the cops. You had found out about the things that [HR "Bob"] Haldeman [the White House Chief of Staff] and [John] Ehrlichman [Nixon's chief domestic advisor] had done but there is no evidence anywhere of a rebuke. But only of scenarios and excuses et cetera. Nowhere do you say we must get this information direct to whomever: the head of the justice

Newscaster David Frost (right) interviews former president Richard Nixon for his television program *Frost on America* in April 1977. (John Bryson/Time & Life Pictures/Getty Images.)

department criminal investigation or whatever. And no-where do you say to Haldeman and Ehrlichman, "This is disgraceful conduct."

Well, could I take my time now to address that question. I think it will be very useful to you to know what I was going through. It wasn't a very easy time. Here was the situation I was faced with: Who's going to talk to these men [Ehrlichman and Haldeman]? What can we do about it? Well, first let me say that I didn't have anyone who could talk to them but me. It took me two weeks to work it out, tortuous long sessions, hours and hours of talks with them, which they resisted—we don't need to go through all that agony. And I remember the day at Camp David when they came up. Haldeman came in first. He said, "I disagree with your decision totally." He said, "I think it's going to eventually . . . you're going to live to regret it, but I will." Ehrlichman then came in. I knew that Ehrlichman was bitter because he felt very strongly that he shouldn't resign. Although he had even indicated that perhaps Haldeman should go and he should stay.

I said, "You know, John [Ehrlichman], when I went to bed last night I hoped, I almost prayed, that I wouldn't wake up this morning." Well, it was an emotional moment; I think there were tears in our eyes, both of us. He said, "Don't say that." We went back in, and they agreed to leave. It was late, but I did it. I cut off one arm and then cut off the other.

Now, I can be faulted; I recognise it. Maybe I defended them too long, maybe I tried to help them too much, but I was concerned about them, I was concerned about their families. I felt that they, and their hearts felt that they, were not guilty. I felt they ought to have a chance at least to prove that they were not guilty. And I didn't want to be in the position of just sawing them off in that way.

And I suppose you could sum it all up the way one of your British prime ministers summed it up, [William Ewart] Gladstone, when he said that the first requirement for a prime minister is to be a good butcher. Well, I think, as far as summary of Watergate is concerned, I did some of the big things rather well. I screwed up terribly on what was a little thing and became a big thing, but I will have to admit I wasn't a good butcher.

> I screwed up terribly on what was a little thing and became a big thing.

You have explained how you have got caught up in this thing, you've explained your motives: I don't want to quibble about any of that. But just coming to the substance: would you go further than "mistakes"—the word that seems not enough for people?

What word would you suggest?

My goodness, that's a . . . I think that there are three things, since you asked me. I would like to hear you say . . . I think the American people would like to hear you say . . . One is: there was probably more than mistakes; there was wrongdoing, whether it was a crime or not; yes it may have been a crime too. Second: I did—and I'm saying this without questioning the motives—I did abuse the power I had as president, or not fulfil the totality of the oath of office. And third: I put the American people through two years of needless agony and I apologise for that. And I say that you've explained your motives, I think those are the categories. And I know how difficult it is for anyone, and most of all you, but I think that people need to hear it and I think unless you say it you are going to be haunted by it for the rest of your life.

I well remember when I let Haldeman and Ehrlichman know that they were to resign, that I had Ray Price

[Nixon's speechwriter] bring in the final draft of the speech that I was to make the next night and I said to him, "Ray, if you think I ought to resign, put that in too, because I feel responsible." Even though I did not feel that I had engaged in these activities consciously in so far as the knowledge of, or participation in, the break-in, the approval of hush-money, the approval of clemency etc, there are various charges that have been made. Well, he didn't put it in, and I must say that at that time I seriously considered whether I shouldn't resign, but on the other hand I feel that I owe it to history, to point out that from that time on April 30 [1973], until I resigned on August 9, I did some things that were good for this country. We had the second and third summits. I think one of the major reasons I stayed in office, was my concern about keeping the China initiative, the Soviet initiative, the Vietnam fragile peace agreement and then an added dividend, the first breakthrough in moving toward—not love, but at least not war—in the Middle East. And, coming back to the whole point of whether I should have resigned then and how I feel now, let me say I didn't make mistakes in just this period; I think some of my mistakes that I regret most deeply came with the statements that I made afterwards. Some of those statements were misleading. I noticed, for example, the managing editor of the *Washington Post*, Ben Bradlee, wrote, a couple, three months ago, as far as his newspaper was concerned: "We don't print the truth; we print what we know, we print what people tell us and this means that we print lies."

I would say that the statements that I made afterwards were, on the big issues, true—that I was not involved in the matters that I have spoken about; not involved in the break-in; that I did not engage in, and participate in, or

> I owe it to history, to point out that . . . I did some things that were good for this country.

approve the payment of money, or the authorisation of clemency, which of course were the essential elements of the cover-up—that was true. But, the statements were misleading in that enormous political attack I was under: it was a five-front war with a fifth column. I had a partisan senate committee staff, we had a partisan special prosecutor's staff, we had a partisan media, we had a partisan judiciary committee staff, and a fifth column. Now under these circumstances, my reactions and some of these statements, from press conferences and so forth after that, I want to say right here and now, I said things that were not true. Most of them were fundamentally true on the big issues, but without going as far as I should have gone and saying perhaps that I had considered other things, but not done them. And for all those things I have a very deep regret.

Only Some Problems Are Admitted

You got caught up in something and it snowballed?

It snowballed, and it was my fault. I'm not blaming anybody else. I'm simply saying to you that as far as I'm concerned, I not only regret it. I indicated my own beliefs in this matter when I resigned. People didn't think it was enough to admit mistakes; fine. If they want me to get down and grovel on the floor; no, never. Because I don't believe I should. On the other hand there are some friends who say, "just face 'em down. There's a conspiracy to get you." There may have been. I don't know what the CIA had to do. Some of their shenanigans have yet to be told, according to a book I read recently. I don't know what was going on in some Republican, some Democratic circles as far as the so-called impeachment lobby was concerned. However, I don't go with the idea that there . . . that what

> I brought myself down. I gave them a sword, and they stuck it in and they twisted it with relish.

brought me down was a coup, a conspiracy etc. I brought myself down. I gave them a sword, and they stuck it in and they twisted it with relish. And I guess if I had been in their position, I'd have done the same thing.

Could you just say, with conviction, I mean not because I want you to say it, that you did do some covering up. We're not talking legalistically now; I just want the facts. You did do some covering up. There was some time when you were overwhelmed by your loyalties or whatever else, you protected your friends, or maybe yourself. In fact you were, to put it at its most simple, part of a cover-up at times.

No, I again respectfully will not quibble with you about the use of the terms. However, before using the term I think it's very important for me to make clear what I did not do and what I did do and then I will answer your question quite directly. I did not in the first place commit the crime of obstruction of justice, because I did not have the motive required for the commission of that crime.

We disagree on that.

I did not commit, in my view, an impeachable offence. Now, the House has ruled overwhelmingly that I did. Of course, that was only an indictment, and it would have to be tried in the Senate. I might have won, I might have lost. But even if I had won in the Senate by a vote or two, I would have been crippled. And in any event, for six months the country couldn't afford having the president in the dock in the United States Senate. And there can never be an impeachment in the future in this country without a president voluntarily impeaching himself. I have impeached myself. That speaks for itself.

> Let me say, if I intended to cover up, believe me, I'd have done it.

How do you mean "I have impeached myself"?

By resigning. That was a voluntary impeachment. Now, what does that mean in terms of whether I . . . you're wanting me to say that I participated in an illegal cover-up. No. Now when you come to the period, and this is the critical period, when you come to the period of March 21 on, when Dean gave his legal opinion, that certain things, actions taken by, Haldeman, Ehrlichman, [attorney general John] Mitchell et cetera, and even by himself amounted to illegal cover-ups and so forth, then I was in a very different position. And during that period, I will admit, that I started acting as lawyer for their defence. I will admit, that acting as lawyer for their defence, I was not prosecuting the case. I will admit that during that period, rather than acting primarily in my role as the chief law enforcement officer of the United States of America, or at least with the responsibility of law enforcement, because the attorney general is the chief law enforcement officer, but as the one with the chief responsibility for seeing that the laws of the United States are enforced, that I did not meet that responsibility. And to the extent that I did not meet that responsibility, to the extent that within the law, and in some cases going right to the edge of the law in trying to advise Ehrlichman and Haldeman and all the rest in how best to present their cases, because I thought that they were legally innocent, that I came to the edge. And under the circumstances I would have to say that a reasonable person could call that a cover-up. I didn't think of it as a cover-up. I didn't intend it to cover-up.

Let me say, if I intended to cover up, believe me, I'd have done it. You know how I could have done it so easy? I could have done it immediately after the election simply by giving clemency to everybody. And the whole thing would have gone away. I couldn't do that because I said clemency was wrong. But now we come down to the key point, and let me answer it in my own way about how I feel about the American people. I mean about whether I should have resigned earlier or what I should say to them now. Well, that forces me to rationalise now and give you a carefully prepared and cropped statement. I didn't expect this question, frankly though, so I'm not going to give you that. But I can tell you this . . .

Nor did I.

I can tell you this. I think I said it all in one of those moments that you're not thinking sometimes you say the things that are really in your heart. When you're thinking in advance and you say things that are, you know, tailored to the audience. I had a lot of difficult meetings in those last days and the most difficult one, the only one where I broke into tears frankly except for that very brief session with Ehrlichman up at Camp David, that was the first time I cried since Eisenhower died. I met with all of my key supporters just the half-hour before going on television. For 25 minutes we all sat around the Oval Office, men that I had come to Congress with, Democrats and Republicans, about half and half. Wonderful men. And at the very end, after saying thank you for all your support during these tough years, thank you particularly for what you have done to help us end the draft, bring home the POWs, have a chance for building a generation of peace, which I could see the dream I had possibly being shattered, and thank you for your friendship, little acts of friendship over the years, you sort of remember with a birthday card and all the rest. Then suddenly you haven't got much more to say and half the people around the table were crying. And I just can't stand seeing somebody else cry. And

> Yep, I let the American people down. And I have to carry that burden with me for the rest of my life.

that ended it for me. And I just, well, I must say I sort of cracked up. Started to cry, pushed my chair back.

And then I blurted it out. And I said, "I'm sorry. I just hope I haven't let you down." Well, when I said: "I just hope I haven't let you down," that said it all. I had: I let down my friends, I let down the country, I let down our system of government and the dreams of all those young people that ought to get into government but will think it is all too corrupt and the rest. Most of all I let down an opportunity I would have had for two and a half more years to proceed on great projects and programmes for building a lasting peace. Which has been my dream, as you know since our first interview in 1968 before I had any, when I thought I might win that year. I didn't tell you I thought I might not win that year, but I wasn't sure. Yep, I let the American people down. And I have to carry that burden with me for the rest of my life. My political life is over. I will never yet, and never again, have an opportunity to serve in any official position. Maybe I can give a little advice from time to time. And so I can only say that in answer to your question that while technically I did not commit a crime, an impeachable offence—these are legalisms. As far as the handling of this matter is concerned, it was so botched up, I made so many bad judgments. The worst ones mistakes of the heart rather than mistakes of the head, as I pointed out, but let me say a man in that top judge job, he's got to have a heart, but his head must always rule his heart.

The Watergate Cover-Up Almost Succeeded

John J. Sirica

In early 1973 the author of the following viewpoint was the judge presiding over the trial that found a group of men guilty of federal charges related to the break-in at the Democratic National Committee headquarters at the Watergate complex. He explains that, as he sat in his office pondering what sentences to give the defendants, he did not know that the burglary had been part of a high-level conspiracy involving President Richard Nixon. Then, in a stunning breach of criminal-case procedures, one of the defendants, James McCord, walked in and gave the judge a sealed envelope. Concerned that the envelope might contain a bribe or in some way involve a setup, he took steps to open the envelope in the presence of witnesses, and to enter its contents, a letter, into the official record. The letter, the author explains, indicated that a cover-up had been attempted and perjury had been committed. He describes the letter as "the beginning of the end" of the Watergate

SOURCE. John J. Sirica, "The McCord Letter," *To Set the Record Straight*, W.W. Norton & Company, 1979, pp. 91–116. Copyright © 1979 by John Sirica Jr. All rights reserved. Reprinted by permission of SLL/Sterling Lord Literistic Inc.

affair. John J. Sirica was a lawyer in Washington, D.C., before being appointed as a federal judge in the district, where he served from 1957 to 1986.

I was far from alone in my skepticism about the facts brought out at the trial. The Senate of the United States had voted to investigate the Republican campaign tactics. The press was full of caustic comment about the trial itself and the government's handling of it. I had been practicing law for thirty years. I had handled cases involving political scandals. I had seen cover-ups in operation before. I had been chief counsel to a congressional committee and had quit when the matter was whitewashed and the investigation stifled. I was often described as an "obscure federal judge," and that was true, but I was not a damn fool. I brought along years of trial experience when I came to the bench back in 1957. I knew the Watergate case was not what the trial in January [1973] had made it seem. But by late March, with the trial over, there didn't seem a lot more I could do about it.

There were many things I didn't know at that time. I didn't know that thousands of dollars had been paid to the very defendants who had just appeared before me, to keep their mouths shut. I didn't know that such a pleasant and successful man as Jeb Magruder, the second-ranking official at the Committee to Re-elect the President, had actually committed perjury in my courtroom to protect himself and his boss, the former attorney general of the United States, John Mitchell. I didn't even begin to think that the president of the United States, Richard Nixon, a man for whom I had campaigned twice when he was running for vice-president, had ordered, within days of the break-in in June 1972, the very cover-up that now had me angry and frustrated.

There were people who already thought I had gone too far during the trial in trying to get the truth out.

Some believe that a federal judge should sit quietly by, like an umpire at a ball game, and make sure the trial runs smoothly, simply ruling on objections raised by the attorneys. I knew the case would go to the court of appeals in the event of a conviction, because of the way I had handled myself, but I have never believed I should sit through a trial with one eye cocked toward the court of appeals. They can tell you after the fact whether you made a mistake, but they can't tell you how to conduct a fair trial at the moment when you have to make a decision from the bench. I have always wanted trials over which I presided to be above all fair—fair to the defendants, to the government, and to the public. The trial of the original Watergate defendants was fair to the defendants and the government, but it didn't seem to me to have been fair to the public. They were asked to believe a theory about how our election process had been corrupted that made no sense to me whatsoever.

On Tuesday morning, March 20, I was working on what at the time I thought would be one of my last tasks in the Watergate case. I had scheduled the sentencing of the defendants for that Friday and had already decided that in one last attempt to get the truth out, I was going to impose provisional sentences on five defendants who had pleaded guilty. I planned to tell them that one factor in determining their final sentences would be their cooperation with the Senate committee, the grand jury, and the prosecutors. I had given up on [G. Gordon] Liddy, who had napped and grinned his way through his own trial. I was going to give him a tough sentence. Also, I was prepared to give [James] McCord a substantial sentence. The courthouse press had dubbed me "Maximum John," a nickname Harry Rosenthal of the Associated Press told me had been coined by a lawyer who had never appeared in my court. It was true that, unlike some other judges, I didn't believe in giving white-collar criminals lighter sentences than others. Maybe the chance to avoid some time in jail, I thought, would jog the memories of [E. Howard] Hunt and the others. It was the day after my sixty-ninth birthday, and although I was still upset by the way the trial had gone, I was looking forward to the end of the case and to getting a little rest.

A Visitor Provides a Shock

At about one thirty that afternoon, I opened the door to the reception room to give a message to my secretary, Mrs. Alease Holley. As I walked through the doorway I saw one of my law clerks, Richard Azzaro, standing in Mrs. Holley's office talking to James McCord. I was shocked. I have a strict policy of not meeting with defendants in criminal cases. Any improper contact between me and a defendant could lead to a mistrial.

> Here was McCord, whose jail sentence I had just been writing, right in my office.

And here was McCord, whose jail sentence I had just been writing, right in my office.

McCord looked like a modestly successful businessman. He was wearing a conservative suit, white shirt, and dark tie. His demeanor suggested that of a salesman who had come to call on a prospective customer, not a man whose future hung in the balance, who faced the prospect of going to jail, who feared that he was being manipulated by powerful people for their own purposes.

He stood calmly beside Mrs. Holley's desk, his back to the door which opened out to another small anteroom; this in turn opened onto the long corridor that led away from my office. He was not at all surprised to see me or nervous in my presence. I motioned to Azzaro to come into my chambers. "What the hell's going on out there?" I asked. My policy against talking to defendants included the law clerks, and they knew it.

Azzaro explained that McCord had walked into the office alone and unannounced. McCord had said he wanted to talk to me, but Azzaro put him off with a small untruth about my being out to lunch. Azzaro also told him that I never spoke to defendants, especially, he added nervously, to convicted criminals. McCord was calm and under total control, and true to his CIA and FBI training and background, gave away none of his emotions. McCord produced a white envelope and asked that it be given to me. His lawyer, McCord told Azzaro, was not aware that he was trying to see me.

> The first thing that came to my mind was that I was being set up by McCord.

I had come up through the rough-and-tumble police and criminal courts in Washington during the 1920's and 1930's, defending and prosecuting at one time or another gamblers and rum runners. Although it may seem improbable now in the fairly strict and orderly atmosphere of a federal court, the first thing that came to my mind was that I was being set up by McCord. "Suppose," I thought, "he has ten thousand dollars' worth of those famous hundred-dollar bills in that envelope and is trying to make it look as though I were accepting a bribe?" In the light of what we now know was going on to maintain the cover-up, perhaps my instinct wasn't so far off.

I told Azzaro to send McCord to his lawyer or to his probation officer with whatever message he was trying to deliver. I called the U.S. attorney's office to get Earl Silbert, who was prosecuting the Watergate case, and his boss, Harold Titus. I was still worried about protecting myself, and I thought, "Hell, I can't do any better than to call the U.S. attorney."

Within an hour, James D. Morgan, a probation officer, had delivered McCord's envelope to my chambers. Silbert and Titus had come to my chambers. I called in my court reporter, Nicholas Sokal, and my two law clerks, Azzaro and Todd Christofferson, as witnesses. We carefully described McCord's visit, so that Sokal could make an official record of what had happened. Titus and Silbert, however, quickly excused themselves from the proceeding. They felt that since McCord's own attorney wasn't there, it would not be proper for them to stay. I asked them to wait in the reception room outside my chambers. Later, I was glad they had left.

The Envelope Is Opened

During my years on the bench, I had tried to discipline myself never to display emotion, for fear of letting the jury know how I was reacting to witnesses. My clerks say I kept a poker face as I opened McCord's envelope. But inside, I was anything but calm.

The envelope contained two letters. The first was disappointing. It was a copy of a letter McCord had written to the *New York Times* denying a story they had published the day before linking him to "strong arm tactics." I never figured out whether McCord wanted me to know the story was in error or whether he included it by mistake.

The second letter was addressed to me. It was neatly typed, with only a few errors, on McCord's white stationery. I read it silently to myself first, maintaining my poker face, but I flushed as I realized what McCord was saying. Then I read it aloud:

> Certain questions have been posed to me from Your Honor through the Probation Officer, dealing with details of the case, motivations, intent, mitigating circumstances. In endeavoring to respond to these questions I am whipsawed in a variety of legalities.
>
> First, I may be called before a Senate Committee investigating this matter.
>
> Secondly, I may be involved in a civil suit.
>
> Thirdly, there may be a new trial at some future date.
>
> Fourthly, the Probation Officer may be called before the Senate Committee to present testimony regarding

> "McCord was going to talk, to break the silence that had frustrated me and millions in the country."

what may otherwise be a privileged communication between defendant and judge, as I understand it.

If I answered certain questions to the Probation Officer it is possible such answers could become a matter of record in the Senate and therefore available for use in the other proceedings just described. My answers would, it would seem to me, violate my Fifth Amendment rights and possibly my Sixth Amendment rights to counsel and possibly other rights. On the other hand, to fail to answer your questions may appear to be noncooperation and I can therefore expect a much more severe sentence.

There are further considerations which are not to be lightly taken. Several members of my family have expressed fear for my life if I disclose knowledge of the facts in this matter either publicly or to any government representatives. Whereas I do not share their concerns to the same degree, nevertheless, I do believe retaliatory measures will be taken against me, my family and my friends should I disclose such facts. Such retaliation could destroy careers, income and reputation of persons who are innocent of any guilt whatever.

Be that as it may, in the interest of justice and in the interest of restoring faith in the criminal justice system which faith had been severely damaged in this case I will state the following to you at this time which I hope may be of help to you in meting out justice in this case.

It was clear McCord was going to talk, to break the silence that had frustrated me and millions in the country ever since the break-in itself. I began to think, "This is it, this is it, this is the break I've been hoping for." I read on:

1. There was political pressure applied to the defendants to plead guilty and remain silent.

2. Perjury occurred during the trial of matters highly material to the very structure, orientation, and impact of the government's case and to the motivation of and intent of the defendants.

3. Others involved in the Watergate operation were not identified during the trial when they could have been by those testifying.

4. The Watergate operation was not a CIA operation. The Cubans may have been misled by others into believing it was a CIA operation. I know for a fact that it was not.

5. Some statements were unfortunately made by a witness which left the Court with the impression that he was stating untruths or withholding facts of his knowledge when in fact only honest errors were involved.

6. My motivations were different than those of the others involved but were not limited to or simply those offered in my defense during the trial. This is not the fault of my attorneys but of the circumstances under which we had to prepare my defense.

I would appreciate the opportunity to talk with you privately in chambers. Since I cannot feel confident in talking with an FBI agent, in testifying before a grand jury whose U.S. Attorneys work for the Department of Justice, or in talking with other government representatives, such a discussion with you would be of assistance to me. I have not discussed the above with my attorneys as a matter of protection for them. I give this statement freely and voluntarily fully realizing that I may be prosecuted for giving a false statement to a judicial official if the statements herein are knowingly untrue. The statements are true and correct to the best of my knowledge and belief.

As I read McCord's signature, I couldn't wait to get Todd Christofferson alone to talk this over. McCord, although he did not name names and was somewhat vague, was indicating not only that he was ready to expose the cover-up but that the cover-up was so extensive that he didn't even trust the FBI or the prosecutors. I ordered the record of the proceeding in my chambers sealed. I decided immediately that no one else was to know about the letter and instructed all present to remain silent about it. I called Titus and Silbert back into my chambers and told them I had decided to seal the proceeding until I could give it further consideration. I thanked them for coming by, and they left. After everyone else was gone, I looked up at Todd, who was to serve as my right arm throughout the Watergate case, and broke into a big grin. The first thing I noticed about the letter was that it was dated the nineteenth, my birthday.

> This case would never have been broken if McCord . . . had not written the letter to me.

"This is the best damned birthday present I've ever gotten," I said. "I always told you I felt someone would talk. This is going to break this case wide open." . . .

Tension Builds Around the Secret Letter

Sentencing of the break-in defendants had been set for Friday the twenty-third. That occasion was the first opportunity I had to make McCord's letter part of the trial record. That morning, I awoke at three thirty. All of us who knew about the letter were extremely nervous. My law clerk Richard Azzaro was still suspicious of the letter and of McCord. He was a former police officer, trained to take precautions. He ordered Charles Artley, the marshal, to check McCord for weapons and pills prior to the opening of court, fearing that if what occurred in the courtroom didn't please the old CIA man, he would try some dramatic stunt. Artley took McCord into the grim little cell block behind my courtroom and searched him thoroughly.

I tried to be as nonchalant as possible as I entered the courtroom. I said a pleasant good morning and announced that I had a "preliminary matter" to take up. As I stated that I had received a letter from McCord, and asked for the sealed envelope, the courtroom hushed. I've never been in a room so full of people that was so quiet. I began reading the letter in as even a voice as I could manage. Azzaro kept his eyes on McCord, seated in the courtroom. As I read, Azzaro remembers, McCord seemed to slump lower and lower in his chair, as if a great tension had been released. It was clear that I was doing what he wanted; making the matter public. I learned later that McCord hadn't even fully trusted me; he had given Bob Jackson, of the *Los Angeles Times*, a copy of the letter in return for a promise to print it if I didn't take some action.

Four or five minutes passed before I got to McCord's numbered charges about political pressure and perjury. As I worked through them, an excruciating pain began to build directly in the center of my chest. It was nearly more than I could bear, but I couldn't quit before the end of the letter. I finally finished the letter and quickly called for a recess. As I hurried off the bench, the reporters flooded toward the double swinging doors at the back of the courtroom. The dam had broken.

Back in my chambers, I stretched out on a sofa. Harry Kelly, of the *Chicago Tribune*, and Dan Thomasson, of the Scripps-Howard papers, came into the office and urged me to see a doctor. But as I relaxed, the pain subsided. My doctor told me later that I was a victim of fatigue and nervous tension. I felt much better after about twenty minutes and went back to the courtroom to pronounce sentence on Liddy and the other defendants. I put off sentencing McCord at the request of his attorney, who was as surprised as the others by the letter. . . .

Columnist Joseph Kraft wrote that same week, "A sudden flurry of developments has transformed the

Watergate affair from a sideshow into a political bomb that could blow the Nixon Administration apart. . . . What all this means is that the issue is obstruction of justice by a systematic cover-up at the highest levels."

In my opinion, this case would never have been broken if McCord had elected to stand pat and had not written the letter to me. That's my conclusion. Once that letter was made public, the parade of people trying to protect themselves began. This was just the beginning of the end. But there was no stopping it.

Playboy Interview: G. Gordon Liddy

G. Gordon Liddy, interviewed by Eric Norden

G. Gordon Liddy was ready to kill even his friend and Watergate plot partner E. Howard Hunt, because Hunt betrayed President Nixon and his country. There is nothing worse than cowardice, Liddy maintains in the following interview, in which he hews to the concepts of personal and national honor. He tells of terrifying White House counsel John Dean during a chance encounter, and he admits that he contemplated executing Dean with a pencil thrust under his jaw. Such actions would be commendable at a time when the presidency and the nation were in grave danger from left-wing revolutionaries, Liddy contends. G. Gordon Liddy was an FBI agent and a lawyer in New York before working for the Nixon administration and the Committee to Re-Elect the President. Sentenced to twenty years for his part in the Watergate conspiracy, he served about four years before President Jimmy Carter commuted his sentence. Eric Norden is an interviewer and author.

SOURCE. G. Gordon Liddy, "Playboy Interview: G. Gordon Liddy," *Playboy*, October, 1980, pp. 71–79. Copyright © 1980 by Playboy. All rights reserved. Reproduced by permission.

Playboy: *[You] planned to murder one of your old buddies and fellow Waterbugger, E. Howard Hunt. Surely, Hunt was no enemy of this country.*

Liddy: At the risk of belaboring this point . . . I would personally never characterize it as murder, because murder by its very definition is *unjustifiable* homicide, and I never would have considered the act in the first place if I had not deemed it eminently justifiable. Hunt had become an informer, a betrayer of his friends and associates, and to me there is nothing lower on this earth. As Nietzsche put it, there is but one sin—cowardice. Hunt deserved to die.

Playboy: Here was a man who had once been your good friend, who was now broken in mind and body, grief stricken over his wife's death and ground down by the rigors of prison life. And so he violated your code and turned state's witness. Couldn't you have forgiven him that and summoned up sufficient compassion to forget, if not forgive?

Liddy: Forgiveness, as Mark Twain once said, is the fragrance a rose leaves on the boot that has crushed it. But I'm afraid you're being naïve as well as sentimental. It wasn't a question of my personal feelings about Hunt, though God knows if he'd stayed a man, I'd have done everything in my power to help him. It wasn't even a question of my detestation of informers, even though I'd point out that we all went into Watergate with our eyes open, were willing to benefit from success and should have been equally willing to face failure with fortitude. No, the stakes were much higher than that, my friend. Hunt knew too much, not only about Watergate but about other matters of state, including CIA secrets. It seemed perfectly plausible to me that my superiors might wish his elimination, and I was prepared to execute those orders without a moment's doubt or soul-searching.

Playboy: Perhaps it is sentimental, at least in your book, but the question of friendship does seem an important consideration here, since none of your other "targets" were close to you personally, as Hunt had once been. E. M. Forster wrote, "If I had a choice between betraying my country or my friend, I hope I would have the courage to betray my country." Is such a concept totally alien to you?

> I would find betraying a friend as unthinkable as betraying my country.

Liddy: Yes, but only because I *do* value friendship, like personal honor, so highly. I would find betraying a friend as unthinkable as betraying my country, and the conundrum would never arise, because the only time I would turn against a friend would be when he had forfeited that friendship by betraying *our* country. And that, of course, is precisely at the root of my feelings about Hunt.

Playboy: Nixon and the political fortunes of his Administration are not exactly synonymous with the national interests of the United States, are they?

Liddy: Well, under the circumstances, and in the light of what's happened to this nation since—and because— Nixon was forced from office, I think you could make a very good case that the two were so inextricably linked that Hunt's betrayal constituted an act at least of regicide, if not of outright treason.

Playboy: Do you feel the same way about Dean?

Liddy: Yes, but even more strongly. For all of Hunt's weaknesses and failings, it would still be manifestly unfair to place him in the same category as Dean. . . . I wouldn't even talk of him in the same breath, much as I condemn his betrayal. The difference between Hunt and Dean is

G. Gordon Liddy arrives
for his January 1973
trial in Washington.
Liddy was convicted
of breaking into
Democratic Party head-
quarters and planting
microphones in the
Watergate case. (**AP
Photo.**)

the difference between a POW who breaks under torture
and aids the enemy and Judas Iscariot.

*Playboy: You've been alone with Dean only once since he
testified against the White House, and you've said that you
contemplated killing him then. How close did you actually
come?*

Liddy: Oh, it was just a fleeting thought, now one of
those sweet memories that one loves to treasure. God
knows, he would have been no loss. What happened,
actually, was that in October of 1974, Federal marshals
escorted me to the offices of Watergate special prosecu-

tor James Neal for an interview and told me to wait in Neal's office, as he was expected shortly. I went in and shut the door behind me and, lo and behold, there was Dean sitting behind the desk. He looked up and I could have sworn he was about to wet himself. His eyes darted all around the room, but I was between him and the door and I could see that he was absolutely terror-stricken. My first thought was that here was the ideal opportunity to kill the bastard. I saw a pencil on the desk and all it would take was a quick thrust through the underside of his jaw, up through the soft palate and deep inside the brain. And simultaneously, I wondered if this were a setup, if someone had arranged for me to be alone with Dean, anticipating exactly such a denouement. But then, on more somber reflection, I ruled that out. Nixon had been out of office for two months, I had received no instructions from my old superiors and, in any case, his killing could only damage the chances of Mitchell, Mardian and others in their forthcoming trials. No, revenge might be a dish best supped cold, but this was positively stale. The whole thing had just been a weird, stupid error. So I exchanged a few inconsequential remarks with Dean, he stammered a reply and I stepped aside so he could gather his papers and scurry out the door. I think he aged considerably in those three or four minutes. . . .

Playboy: As long as we're on such a murderous topic, is there any such thing as an untraceable poison?

Liddy: Yes, there are a few, in the colloidal family, and they're known—and used by—the intelligence services of the superpowers. But they may not be untraceable for long, since there's recently been a considerable, forensic breakthrough in that area. But generally, you know, even traceable poisons are *not* traced, unless there's reason to suspect foul play. Most autopsies are *pro forma*, unless the forensic pathologist is on his toes and already suspicious; so if you use a poison that simulates the symptoms of heart failure, say, you're generally home safe and dry.

There's a wide range of poisons that can be manufactured simply at home, without complex laboratory technology. Give me several cigars, for example, and in a short while I'll have extracted enough pure nicotine to kill a man with a few drops in his food or coffee. That was how I was going to handle Hunt, in fact, if the signal had come down from on high. But, once again, I don't want to spell out the process in any detail, lest I put ideas into the heads of any impressionable adolescents in your audience.

Playboy: You have one hell of an opinion of the young people across this country.

Liddy: Realism, my friend, realism. If people know how to do something, no matter how nasty, sooner or later somebody's going to do it. It's the nature of the beast. . . .

Playboy: Your critics would contend that you had far more in common with the Mafia than a mutual scorn for stool pigeons—i.e., a dedication to the principle that the ends justify the means.

Liddy: Well, I've never denied that. When the issues are significant enough, the ends *do* justify the means. And, in fact, most people in this society operate on just that assumption, though a lot of them gloss it over with a shimmering veil of hypocrisy, like John Sirica. Didn't *The New York Times* believe that the end justified the means in the Pentagon papers case, when it published purloined top-secret Government documents? And didn't the civil rights and antiwar demonstrators believe that the ends justified the means when they broke the law by sit-ins at lunch counters or burning their draft cards? Sure they did, and at least in the civil rights movement, they were prepared to go to jail for their convictions. It was only when we countered the illegal actions of the antiwar movement with some of our own that they tore their hair and rent their raiments and screamed, "Police state!" and the whole thing turned into a morality play. All a question of whose political ox is getting gored, of course. When I'm in a war, I can respect my opponent, no matter how strongly I detest his convictions. What I cannot stand is hypocrisy.

Playboy: That's the second analogy you've made between your conduct and that of a soldier in wartime, and throughout your trial and imprisonment, you certainly conducted yourself as a POW trapped in enemy territory. If you were a soldier, weren't your only enemies fellow Americans of differing political views?

Liddy: That's easy enough to believe if you conveniently distort the facts of recent history. Everybody today knows that in the late Sixties and early Seventies, we were involved in an exterior war in Vietnam, but they tend to forget that we were also embroiled in an undeclared civil war at home. And unless you can understand the nature of that struggle and the issues it posed for the Administration in Washington, you'll never be able to understand my motives or the motives of my associates in undertaking the actions and running the risks we did. We were up against a formidable constellation of forces in those days. . . . It was as unthinkable to me to let the country succumb to those values as it would have been for a Japanese officer reared on the code of *Bushido* to contemplate surrender in 1945.

> We were also embroiled in an undeclared civil war at home.

Playboy: And so you became a kamikaze, and ultimately self-destructed over Watergate?

Liddy: No. I joined people who believed as I did in a well-justified counter-offensive against the forces of civil disorder that were sweeping the country in those days. And I have absolutely no regrets about my decision to do so. Ultimately, our side won out and crushed the revolutionaries, which is one salient reason why what's left of the left has never forgotten or forgiven Richard Nixon. But our very victory has to some extent obscured the gravity of the situation as it was seen in Washington in those days.

Playboy: Aren't you drastically exaggerating the true dimensions of civil unrest in order to justify your own violations of the law? Sure, there were antiwar demonstrations and civil disobedience and some incidents of terrorism by crazies like the Weathermen, but can you seriously argue that the country was teetering on the brink of a revolutionary upheaval?

> " I remembered Cicero's dictum that laws are inoperative in war. "

Liddy: In my opinion, you're seriously *under*estimating the threat. We didn't have a crystal ball at our disposal in those days that would inform us that mass student opposition to the war would peter out after the end of the draft, or that, the racial cauldron in the big cities would eventually simmer down. We had to act on our best intelligence assessment of the forces arrayed against us, and that assessment was far from encouraging, particularly when you consider the revolutionaries. Remember, we knew that those same forces had caused Lyndon Johnson to abdicate his office, and we were not prepared to see a similar scenario in the case of Richard Nixon. We drew the line and chose to fight back.

Playboy: You never had any doubts that the antiwar movement posed a serious threat to this country and its institutions?

Liddy: Never for a moment. They were the shock troops of a movement and value system I despised, and as far as I was concerned, if they were going to succeed, they would have had to march over my dead body. And I always felt justified in taking any action necessary to thwart them. I remembered Cicero's dictum that laws are inoperative in war. And I knew we were at war.

The White House Counsel Has an Odd Encounter with Nixon

John W. Dean III

As assertions grew about a White House cover-up, Richard Nixon summoned John Dean to a one-on-one meeting, Dean relates in the following viewpoint. There, the president led Dean through an odd conversation in which Nixon presented a defense of himself, almost as if someone were listening in judgment. Only later did Dean learn of Nixon's secret audio recording system. In the conversation, Dean warned Nixon that the White House was vulnerable to legal charges of obstruction of justice. The next morning, Dean was summoned again, and this time the president suggested Dean sign two incriminating letters of resignation. John Dean, a lawyer, rose in the federal government to become White House legal counsel in 1970. After serving four months in prison for

SOURCE. John W. Dean III, "Scrambling," *Blind Ambition*, Simon and Schuster, 1976, pp. 258–267. Copyright © 1976 by John W. Dean. All rights reserved. Reproduced by permission.

obstruction of justice in the Watergate scandal, he became a writer and investment banker.

At nine-fifteen [P.M.] on Sunday, April 15 [1973], a Secret Service agent outside the President's Executive Office Building office told me to go right in. I found the President seated in his easy chair in the far corner of his large office, both feet up on the ottoman. He had on what appeared to be a smoking jacket. As I sat down near him, on one of the conference-table chairs, I was close enough to notice a smell of liquor on his breath. He seemed exhausted. His usually neatly creased trousers looked as if he had slept in them, and his necktie was stained. This was not the well-manicured Richard Nixon I was used to.

"Would you like something to drink? Scotch? Martini? Anything?" he asked. The President had never before offered me a drink.

"No, thank you, sir."

"Come on, you'll surely have something?" It was almost an order and I didn't feel I could refuse it.

"I'll have a Coke, thank you." He buzzed his valet, told him I would have a Coke, he would have coffee.

When the valet left, I told the President what was bothering me. "Mr. President, I don't know if you've been told, but I have talked with the prosecutors . . ."

"Yes, [Richard] Kleindienst and [Henry] Petersen were here to see me today."

"Uh, well, I wanted to tell you I was going to the prosecutors. I hoped to tell you before you learned from somebody else. And, uh, I didn't feel when I went to them that I was doing it out of any disloyalty to you, I assure you, Mr. President. I hope someday you'll know I was being loyal to you when I did this. I, uh, felt it was the only way to end the cover-up. And so I thought I had to tell them that I knew, Mr. President, and now I think you're in a position where you can step out in front of it."

The President Poses Questions

The President was nodding affirmatively. He seemed quite friendly. "I understand, John," he said. "I want you to know I understand." He paused. Maybe it will work, I thought. "I'd kind of like to review some of these problem areas that have come up. I'd like to go over them a little bit with you." He looked down at the legal pad on his lap. "For example, let's get into a little bit of this money problem. I'm trying to sort it out, you understand. Let's take [John] Ehrlichman. What's Ehrlichman's involvement in that?"

"Well, Mr. President, both Bob [Haldeman] and John guided me in this area every inch of the way. I went to John after [John] Mitchell asked for help on the funds, and I asked John if he thought it was all right to use [Nixon's personal attorney Herbert] Kalmbach. I went to him several times, and he approved. Both John and Bob. That's what they did. Uh, they saw the need for it, and then I went to Kalmbach."

> I was between suspicion and hope. I thought the President was, too.

The President nodded. "I understand. Now, what about Petersen? How deep is Henry in this thing?"

This question surprised me. I hesitated before answering. Maybe the President just wanted to make sure Petersen was impartial enough to be his counsel on the matter, as I had suggested. On the other hand, maybe the President was probing for evidence of Petersen's own involvement, to use it as leverage to keep Henry from pursuing the cover-up. I was between suspicion and hope. I thought the President was, too. "Well, Mr. President, uh, as I've told you, Henry kept me posted on this thing. He did tell me at one point, for example, that [Jeb] Magruder

Nixon aide John Dean, with his wife Maureen behind him, testifies before the Senate committee conducting hearings on the Watergate break-in. **(Steve Northup/Time Life Pictures/Getty Images.)**

had made it through the grand jury 'by the skin of his teeth.' But I don't think Henry would be what you'd call deep into the thing. I think he's well aware of the problem areas. And I think that you could well take your counsel from him. He knows all the ramifications, and I think he's the best man to help protect you."

> So what? I thought finally. What difference does it make if I admit my involvement?

"Well," said the President, "you know Petersen questions Haldeman for not cutting this [G. Gordon] Liddy plan off originally. He says that when you came back from that second meeting with Mitchell and you came back and told Bob about this crazy scheme Liddy was planning—uh, what *did* Bob tell you then, John?"

"Well, he said I should have nothing to do with it, and I felt the plan had been killed then. I really did."

"That's right." The President frowned. "That's what I understand the facts are. But Petersen says, 'Well, why didn't Haldeman do something about it?' He doesn't like that."

I could see the President's worry for Haldeman, and was encouraged at the signs that he recognized how seriously Bob was involved.

The President went back to Petersen, raising Henry's suggestion that the President encourage Liddy to come forward with the facts. I agreed. The President then called Petersen to discuss the idea, winking at me when he told Petersen I had "stepped out for a minute."

I was encouraged as I listened to the President's end of the conversation. He was telling Petersen that he would urge Liddy to come forward. He was following my counsel. I couldn't tell whether the President was protecting himself with Petersen or genuinely moving to do the right thing, but I longed to give him the benefit of the doubt.

The Questioning Seems Odd

When the call ended, however, the President aroused my suspicions again. He looked down at his pad and resumed his questions about the facts, focusing on my own involvement, my own legal weaknesses. Each time I told him what they were, he would say, "Now, John, I want you to tell the truth about that when you're questioned, understand?" "Yes, sir," I would reply, but my mind was elsewhere. I was studying him. He is posturing himself, I thought—always placing his own role in an innocuous perspective and seeking my agreement. I wondered if the meeting was a setup. Was he recording me? I noticed a small cassette recorder on the table beside him, but it wasn't running. I glanced around the room, looking for a machine somewhere else. My hopes wrestled my mistrust to a draw. So what? I thought finally. What difference does it make if I admit my involvement?

"Well, John," he said after running through his list of questions, "what's your counsel on whether I should keep Haldeman and Ehrlichman on? I think that's an issue that I'd like to have your advice on. Uh, I've been talking with Petersen about it, and he thinks maybe they should be removed."

I was surprised by the question. The President did not seem to be posturing. Maybe he was seriously weighing this option. My hopes rose again. "Uh, frankly, Mr. President, I would follow Petersen's advice on that. I really can't see any alternative, you know, to protect the Presidency."

The President shook his head sadly. "You think their problems are that bad, eh?"

"Well, I'm afraid so, yes. I think they are at least as bad as my own," I replied, restraining myself. "My lawyer and I have gone over these obstruction statutes, Mr. President, and you'd be surprised by them. They are as broad as the imagination of man, and I'm convinced all of us have serious legal problems."

The President sighed. "What about you, John? Are you prepared to resign?"

"I have thought a lot about that, Mr. President, and I am. I'm not happy about it, but I think it has to occur. I want you to know I'm ready when you say so."

"Good." He nodded. "Good. Let me say this, John. I'm not happy about this, but Petersen has been talking to me about it. It is a painful thing for the President, you know. I don't think it's fair. I don't think it's right. But what can you say?" He looked off helplessly.

"I understand, Mr. President, but I want you to know I understand the important thing is the Presidency."

"That's right," he said.

"That's what matters."

"That's right." The President looked at me, paused, and then spoke in a soft, quiet voice. "John, let me ask you this. Have you talked to the prosecutors at all about your conversations with the President?"

"No, sir, Mr. President," I replied immediately. "I haven't even talked to my lawyer about anything in that area. Those are in privileged areas, as far as I'm concerned."

"That's right," he said, nodding vigorously. "And I don't want you talking about national-security matters, or, uh, executive-privilege things. Uh, those newsmen's wiretaps and things like that—those are privileged, John. Those are privileged. Not that there's anything wrong with them, understand. But they're national security. There's no doubt about that."

"I agree, Mr. President." I knew he was protecting himself with this admonition, but I didn't care. That was my purpose as well.

> Now I knew [Nixon] was posturing that he'd known nothing about Watergate until that day.

The President sat up slowly, removing his feet from the ottoman and placing his pad on it. "John, do you remember that conversation when you came in and told me about, you know, the cancer on the Presidency and things like that?"

"Yes, sir." I wondered what he was driving at.

"Well, let me ask you something. When *was* that?"

"Well, let me think. I can't put a date on it off the top of my head, but I know it was the Wednesday just before Hunt was sentenced. It wouldn't be hard to find out."

"Good," he said. "Would you check on that for me? That's when you brought the facts in to me for the first time, isn't it? And gave me the whole picture?"

"Yes, sir, it is." Now I knew he was posturing that he'd known nothing about Watergate until that day. It was a lie, but it was all right with me as long as he didn't do so at my expense. I couldn't tell which way he was going.

Mistakes Are Seen as Jokes

The President leaned over toward me, and a mischievous look came across his face. "You know, that mention I made to you about a million dollars and so forth as no problem . . ." He laughed softly. "I was just joking, of course, when I said that."

I smiled and nodded as the President rose to his feet with some effort and stretched briefly. "Well, Mr. President, I'm not even getting into those areas. You can be assured of that."

"Good," he said, looking down at me. He began walking slowly, circling around my chair toward the window. "You know, John, this guy [E. Howard] Hunt has caused us a lot of problems, but I can kind of understand how sad it is for him. You know, with his wife dead, and being in jail like that. Awfully tough. I really feel sorry for him, and it's hard to look at his situation objectively." The President stopped in the corner behind his chair, about ten feet away from me. He paused and looked out the window toward the lights on the West Wing of the White House, his arms folded in front of him. Then he looked over at me. "John," he said in a hushed tone, "I guess it was foolish of me to talk to [Charles] Colson about clemency. Uh, wasn't it?"

I nodded silently and slowly. The President had just mentioned the two most troublesome areas he had dis-

> 'You know, that mention I made to you about a million dollars . . . I was just joking.'

cussed with me. He knew they were his biggest mistakes, but he was telling me that he considered them small ones—jokes, little errors.

His spirits suddenly picked up again. "Well, John, I want to thank you for coming in here tonight. I want you to think about these things, and we'll talk again about them soon, maybe tomorrow."

"Thank you, Mr. President," I said, rising. "I will think about them. I feel a lot better after this conversation." And I did feel better. At least the President had not exploded at me, called me a Judas, fired me, announced a new cover-up. . . .

I drove home, turning the conversation over and over in my mind. Everything could be interpreted many ways. At least I didn't feel humiliated or repudiated. The cover-up was hanging in the balance. Maybe the President *would* thank me for what I had done. Maybe he was plotting to screw me to the wall. I knew that was a possibility. For the rest of the evening I wavered back and forth, slowly drowning my worries in alcohol, imagining Nixon doing the same.

The Next Morning Proves Chilling

The President summoned me to his office first thing the next morning, April 16. As I walked over to the West Wing my mind was nearly blank; I felt as if I were on automatic pilot. The President would give me some sign of the way he was moving, I knew, but I had no idea how strong it would be. On so many occasions I had seen momentous decisions evaded.

> I looked at the President without expression. He was being sneaky, but he was weak.

Haldeman and Ehrlichman burst out of the Oval Office as I arrived. They were laughing together like college pranksters, but went abruptly straight-faced when they noticed me. The first bad sign. Those were not the looks of men who had been told they had to resign. We exchanged grave nods.

I took a chair to the right of the President's desk, on his left. He greeted me, shuffled some papers nervously. I felt oddly calm by comparison with last night. The President was too worried to explode at me. He now knew what I had done. I thought he was frightened, just as I was.

He came quickly to his point. "You will remember we talked about resignations, et cetera, et cetera, that I should have in hand," he said, waving his hand in an effort to lighten the matter. He paused. "Not to be released."

"Uh huh," I mumbled, as I always did when the President said something I didn't like. We had talked about resignations, indeed, but never about having to have them "in hand." I waited.

"But I should have in hand something, or otherwise they will say, 'What the hell. After Dean told you all of this, what did you do?' You see?"

"Uh huh."

"I talked to Petersen about this other thing, and I said, 'Now, what do you want to do about this situation on Dean, et cetera?' And he said, 'Well, I don't want to announce anything now.' You know what I mean?"

"Uh huh."

"But what is your feeling on that? See what I mean?"

I looked at the President without expression. He was being sneaky, but he was weak, I thought. Stroking me. Asking for my advice. Hoping I'd volunteer to do what he wanted: resign alone. "Well," I said quietly, "I think it ought to be Dean, Ehrlichman and Haldeman."

"Well, I thought Dean for the moment," the President replied, but without much force.

"All right," I said, waiting to hear him out.

"Dean at this moment," he continued, "because you are going to be going, and I will have to handle them also. But the point is . . ." He hesitated as if he had lost the thread. "What is your advice?" Before I could answer, he remembered his next point. "You see, the point is, we just typed up a couple, just to have here, which I would be willing to put out. You know . . ."

A Presentation of Tough Choices

He had finally gotten hold of what I knew he'd been looking for—my letter of resignation. He had two of them, in fact, and he slid them across his desk toward me with a jerky push. As I scanned the first one, the President kept assuring me, unconvincingly, that Haldeman and Ehrlichman had also offered their resignations.

The first letter stunned me.

> Dear Mr. President:
>
> As a result of my involvement in the Watergate matter, which we discussed last night and today, I tender to you my resignation effective at once.

No wonder he's so nervous, I thought. He's asking me to sign a confession. I saw [press secretary Ron] Ziegler reading this letter in the Press Room. I visualized Judge [John] Sirica announcing that since Liddy had gotten twenty years, I deserved no less than forty. I suppressed the thought and read the second letter. It was worse.

> Dear Mr. President:
>
> In view of my increasing involvement in the Watergate matter, my impending appearance before the grand jury and the probability of its action, I request an immediate and indefinite leave of absence from my position on your staff.

The President was suggesting that I sign *both* letters. I was shocked. Mechanically, I discussed both letters as if they were drafts of speeches. And, as I did, a debate raged deep inside me. A voice said, The President is undeniably a devious bastard who'll ruin you any way he can. You should lash out at him, tell him what you really think, tell him how to save himself. He'll probably fall off his chair and agree. Another voice said, The President is your whole life. He is vacillating; he is talking about firing Haldeman and Ehrlichman too; he just needs a little push to do the right thing. The voices canceled each other out. I was just strong enough to resist the President, not strong enough to defy him.

> I was just strong enough to resist the President, not strong enough to defy him.

"Uh, what I would like to do," I said, "is draft an alternative letter putting in both options, and you can just put them in the file." Short and sweet.

The President nodded; he backed down as I had expected.

Nixon's Daughter Praises Her Father's Courage

Julie Nixon Eisenhower, interviewed by Larry King

Richard Nixon was humiliated and humbled by the Watergate scandal, his daughter Julie says in the following excerpt from an interview conducted at the Nixon Presidential Library and Museum in Yorba Linda, California. He continued to be positive about life, not bitter, she maintains, but he did feel he let down his friends as well as the country. She tells of the agony of the family's last moments in the White House after years of tumult. She contends that her father did not give up but instead rebuilt his life. Julie Nixon Eisenhower, the second daughter of Richard and Patricia Nixon, has worked as an author and editor. Larry King is a radio and TV host best known for his eponymous talk show that ran on CNN from 1985 to 2010.

*L*arry King: Did he—was he bitter after he left office?

Julie Nixon Eisenhower: He was not bitter. I think he was humiliated and humbled. And he knew that the whole Watergate episode had made a lot of young people cynical about government. He said once that, you know, letting down the American people is a burden I will carry until the day I die.

And all that said, you know, he knew what had happened, what I admire most about him and especially as I get older and I have some times in my life where I think, oh, it is not worth trying to do this, or I don't really want to try to do that, you know he just was so positive about life. He never gave up, Larry. . . .

Well, Julie, this is the Watergate Pavilion [of the Nixon Library], I guess.

Julie Nixon Eisenhower and her husband, David Eisenhower, Betty Ford, and President Gerald Ford (left to right) watch as Richard Nixon departs the White House after his resignation on August 9, 1974. (**AP Photo/Bob Daugherty.**)

> "The Watergate story is not the greatest story, let's put it that way."

We have a long exhibit here, very dense text, so people can stop and read as much as they want. We have two listening stations with the June 23 tape.

The "I am not a crook" speech. Is that here? When [Dan] Rather asks him those questions?

That one is not here.

All the bad side of it is here, right?

Well, all—the Watergate story is not the greatest story, let's put it that way. It is all here, right. . . .

And you know, some of the notes, the decisions that he made, some of the original, agonizing—the photos tell the story. And then of course this—picture that those who lived through the era probably will never forget, the last wave from the helicopter.

Where were you?

I was standing next to President [Gerald] Ford on the South Grounds, David [Eisenhower, her husband] and I were staying behind to help pack up some more things. And my sister [Tricia] and Ed [Cox, Tricia's husband] went on to San Clemente.

Was his farewell speech—you were there, was that the saddest moment in your life?

No. I don't think it was the saddest moment of my life. But, it was a very difficult moment. Because I knew he was in agony, and, again, he felt he had let down his friends. He let down the country, and he was someone who all his life had tried to serve his country, so it was a very tragic end to his presidency. He had done so many good things.

Did you ever fear an impeachment trial? Did you ever think it would happen?

I didn't, I thought it would happen. So the whole thing was agony, but the presidency was a pretty agonizing time because of the war. As I said, Larry, there was never a calm moment. It was—the most tumultuous years you could have ever imagined.

What was this like for you?

Well, this was very difficult, I think I was practically numb at the end. And, finally the helicopter lifted off, and, that was it. But he built his life back again. And that is what matters in life.

CHRONOLOGY

1968   November 5: With less than a majority of the popular vote, Richard M. Nixon wins election as US president. The Republican Nixon is backed by 43.4 percent of the voters, compared to Democrat Hubert H. Humphrey's 42.7 percent and independent George Wallace's 13.5 percent.

1971   June 13: The *New York Times* begins publishing the government's secret history of the Vietnam War, the Pentagon Papers, as the Nixon administration loses court battles to suppress their publication.

September 9: A unit secretly dispatched by the White House burglarizes a psychiatrist's office, seeking files on the leaker of the Pentagon Papers, Daniel Ellsberg.

1972   May 28: A Republican-backed team secretly installs electronic surveillance equipment at the Democrats' National Committee headquarters in the Watergate building complex.

June 17: Five men are arrested at about 2:30 A.M. while trying to place spying devices in the Democrats' Watergate offices. It will later be revealed that the five were directed by the Nixon reelection campaign.

June 23: Without public disclosure, Nixon orders his chief of staff, H.R. Haldeman, to tell the FBI that its investigation of the Watergate break-in must stop because it could endanger national security.

August 29: Nixon declares in a news conference that no one in his administration was involved in the break-in.

October 10: The *Washington Post* reports that FBI agents have found that the Watergate break-in was part of a widespread Nixon reelection campaign of political spying and sabotage.

November 11: Nixon wins reelection by a landslide over Democrat George McGovern, but Democrats retain their majorities in the House of Representatives and Senate.

1973   January 8: A trial begins before US District Judge John Sirica of the men arrested in connection with the Watergate break-in.

January 30: Former Nixon aides G. Gordon Liddy and James McCord Jr. are convicted of burglary, wiretapping, and conspiracy in connection with the Watergate break-in. Five other men plead guilty.

February–March: Nixon and his associates continue denying Watergate involvement.

April 6: White House counsel John W. Dean III begins cooperating with Watergate prosecutors.

April 30: Under pressure from investigations, Nixon's top staff members, H.R. Haldeman and John Ehrlichman, resign, along with US attorney general Richard Kleindienst. Dean is fired. Nixon continues to say he had no prior knowledge of the break-in.

May 18: A US Senate committee begins televised hearings about Watergate. Separately, new attorney general Elliot Richardson announces the appointment of

Archibald Cox as special prosecutor for Watergate.

June 25: Dean tells the Senate committee that Nixon was involved in the cover-up soon after the break-in, and that the Nixon White House conducted political espionage for years.

July 16: Testifying before Congress, former presidential aide Alexander Butterfield reveals that Nixon secretly recorded the conversations and telephone calls in his offices, beginning in February 1971.

July 23: Nixon refuses to give secret tape recordings to the special prosecutor of the Senate Watergate committee. The legal struggle over the tapes continues for months.

August 15: In a televised speech, Nixon denies involvement in the Watergate cover-up.

October 10: Vice President Spiro Agnew resigns and pleads no-contest to a charge that he accepted kickbacks while governor of Maryland.

October 12: Nixon selects Gerald Ford, the leader of the Republican minority in the House of Representatives, to be vice president.

October 20: In what became known as the Saturday Night Massacre, Nixon fires the Watergate special prosecutor, and the attorney general and deputy attorney general resign in protest.

November 1: Leon Jaworski becomes special prosecutor.

November 17: In a press conference, Nixon declares, "I'm not a crook." He adds, "And in all of my years of public life I have never obstructed justice."

November 21: The White House discloses an eighteen-and-a-half-minute gap in a key secret tape recording. Presidential secretary Rose Mary Woods says she probably erased it accidentally.

December 6: After being confirmed by Congress, Ford is sworn in as vice president.

1974   January 4: The Senate Watergate Committee subpoenas more than five hundred tape recordings. Nixon refuses to comply, saying presidential conversations must remain confidential.

April 3: After an IRS investigation, Nixon is forced to pay $432,787 in back taxes.

April 30: The White House gives the House Judiciary Committee edited transcripts of secret recordings, but not the tapes themselves. In the transcripts, "expletive deleted" appears frequently.

July 24: Rejecting the president's claims of executive privilege, the US Supreme Court rules unanimously that Nixon must turn over the recordings of sixty-four White House conversations sought by the special prosecutor.

July 27: The House Judiciary Committee declares that Nixon obstructed justice and votes to impeach him. Over the next few days the committee adds impeachment charges of abuse of power and defiance of its subpoenas.

August 5: Newly released tape recording transcripts (including a June 23, 1972, conversation with Haldeman) show that Nixon ordered the Watergate cover-up less than a week after the break-in. More

Republicans in the House now say they favor impeachment.

August 6: Nixon tells his cabinet that he will not resign.

August 7: Some of Nixon's informed supporters tell him he would not win an impeachment trial.

August 8: Nixon resigns, effective the next day.

August 9: Nixon leaves the White House and heads for his home in California. Ford succeeds him as president.

September 8: Ford grants Nixon a "full, free and absolute" pardon.

FOR FURTHER READING

Books

Richard Ben-Veniste and George Frampton, Jr., *Stonewall: The Real Story of the Watergate Prosecution*. New York: Simon & Schuster, 1977.

Carl Bernstein and Bob Woodward, *All the President's Men*. New York: Simon & Schuster, 1974.

Jimmy Breslin, *How the Good Guys Finally Won: Notes from an Impeachment Summer*. New York: Viking Press, 1975.

William F. Buckley Jr., *Execution Eve—And Other Contemporary Ballads*. New York: Putnam, 1975.

Charles Colson, *Born Again*. Old Tappan, NJ: Chosen Books, 1976.

Congressional Quarterly, *Watergate: Chronology of a Crisis*. Washington, DC: CQ Press, 1973–1974.

Sam Dash, *Chief Counsel: Inside the Ervin Committee—The Untold Story of Watergate*. New York: Random House, 1976.

Maureen Dean, *"Mo": A Woman's View of Watergate*. New York: Simon & Schuster, 1975.

Julie Nixon Eisenhower, *Pat Nixon: The Untold Story*. New York: Simon & Schuster, 1986.

Sam Ervin, *The Whole Truth: The Watergate Conspiracy*. New York: Random House, 1980.

Gerald Ford, *A Time to Heal: The Autobiography of Gerald R. Ford*. New York: Harper & Row, 1979.

H.R. Haldeman, *The Haldeman Diaries: Inside the Nixon White House*. New York: G.P. Putnam's, 1994.

Howard Hunt, with Greg Aunapu, *American Spy: My Secret History in the CIA, Watergate, and Beyond*. Hoboken, NJ: Wiley, 2007.

Leon Jaworski, *The Right and the Power: The Prosecution of Watergate*. New York: Reader's Digest Press, 1976.

Stanley I. Kutler, *The Wars of Watergate: The Last Crisis of Richard Nixon*. New York: Knopf, 1990.

G. Gordon Liddy, *Will: The Autobiography of G. Gordon Liddy*. New York: St. Martin's Press, 1980.

Jeb Stuart Magruder, *An American Life: One Man's Road to Watergate*. New York: Atheneum, 1974.

Frank Mankiewicz, *Perfectly Clear: Nixon from Whittier to Watergate*. New York: Quadrangle/New York Times Book Co., 1973.

Jon Marshall, *Watergate's Legacy and the Press: The Investigative Impulse*. Evanston, IL: Northwestern University Press, 2011.

Mary McCarthy, *The Masks of State: Watergate Portraits by Mary McCarthy*. New York: Harcourt Brace Jovanovich, 1974.

Wizola McLendon, *Martha: The Life of Martha Mitchell*. New York: Random House, 1979.

Richard Nixon, *The Memoirs of Richard Nixon*. New York: Grosset & Dunlap, 1978.

Dan Rather and Gary Paul Gates, *The Palace Guard*. New York: Harper & Row, 1974.

Elliot Richardson, *Reflections of a Radical Moderate*. New York: Pantheon, 1996.

William Safire, *Before the Fall: An Inside View of the Pre-Watergate White House*. Garden City, NY: Doubleday, 1975.

Theodore H. White, *Breach of Faith: The Fall of Richard Nixon*. New York: Atheneum, 1975.

Periodicals

Ben H. Bagdikian, "The Fruits of Agnewism," *Columbia Journalism Review*, January-February 1973.

Marjorie Boyd, "The Watergate Story: Why Congress Didn't Investigate Until After the Election," *Washington Monthly*, April 1973.

William F. Buckley Jr., "Foul Felt," *National Review*, Vol. 57, No. 12, July 4, 2005.

Edward J. Epstein, "Did the Press Uncover Watergate?" *Commentary*, July 1974.

Mark Feldstein, "Watergate Revisited," *American Journalism Review*, vol. 26, no. 4, August–September 2004.

Seymour Hersh, "Watergate Days," *New Yorker*, vol. 81, no. 17, June 13, 2005.

George V. Higgins, "The Judge Who Tried Harder," *Atlantic*, April 1974.

Christopher Hitchens, "Minority Report," *Nation*, vol. 250, no. 25, June 25, 1990.

Carroll Kilpatrick, "Nixon Forces Firing of Cox; Richardson, Ruckelshaus Quit," *Washington Post*, October 21, 1973.

Carroll Kilpatrick, "Nixon Resigns," *Washington Post*, August 9, 1974.

Stanley I. Kutler, "Nixon, Watergate, and History," *New England Journal of History*, vol. 56, nos. 2–3, 1999–2000.

Richard Lyons and William Chapman, "Judiciary Committee Approves Article to Impeach President Nixon, 27 to 11," *Washington Post*, July 28, 1974.

Tod Olson, "The Fall of a President: The Watergate Scandal Changed American Politics Forever," *Scholastic Update*, vol. 129, no. 14, May 2, 1997.

David M. Oshinsky, "Lest We Forget," *New Leader*, vol. 73, no. 8, May 14, 1990.

Charles Peters, "Why the White House Press Didn't Get the Watergate Story," *Washington Monthly*, August-September 1973.

Walter Pincus, "Did Mr. Nixon Mislead the Prosecution?" *Washington Post*, June 8, 1974.

Donnie Radcliffe, "Martha Mitchell: Two Long Years After Watergate," *Washington Post*, June 16, 1974.

Eric Redman, "Pre-Watergate Watch: Did Nixon Legally Win the 1968 Election?" *Rolling Stone*, March 13, 1975.

Evan Thomas, "A Long Shadow; Understanding Deep Throat: Why a Source Took on a President Then, and How Nixon's Fall Shapes Us Even Now," *Newsweek*, June 13, 2005.

"The Last Week: The Unmaking of the President," *Time*, August 19, 1974.

Sanford Ungar, "The FBI File: Men and Machinations in the Court of J. Edgar Hoover," *Atlantic*, April 1975.

Websites

Nixon Library Watergate Archives (www.nixonlibrary.gov). In March 2011, the Watergate Gallery opened at the Nixon Presidential Library and Museum. The library now gives the public access to a wealth of information on the events leading to Richard Nixon's impeachment and resignation. The library's website now includes Watergate-related materials, including secretly recorded conversations in audio and transcript form. They include the infamous "smoking gun" conversation between Nixon and H.R. Haldeman and the "cancer upon the presidency" conversation among Nixon, Haldeman, and John W. Dean III.

The Watergate Story (www.washingtonpost.com). The *Washington Post*, the newspaper that broke the story of the break-in at the Democratic National Headquarters and whose investigative reporting is credited with exposing the events that led to Richard Nixon's resignation, provides an online archive of the major Watergate stories appearing in its pages. The articles are grouped in four sections: The *Post* Investigates, The Government Acts, Nixon Resigns, and Deep Throat Revealed.

Watergate Collection (www.time.com). *Time* provides a web-based archive of articles from the magazine covering the Watergate break-in, the subsequent cover-up, the trial, the vote to impeach Nixon, his resignation, and the scandal's aftermath.

Watergate.Info (www.watergate.info). Created by Australian schoolteacher Malcolm Farnsworth, this unofficial but illuminating site assembles a wealth of Watergate material.

INDEX

Eisenhower, Julie Nixon and, 177
Ervin and, 62
House investigation, 58
Jordan and, 71–76
Nixon/Frost interview and, 138–139, 141
obstruction of justice and, 19–20
petition calling for, *16*
See also Nixon
Income tax audits, 43–44
Internal Revenue Service (IRS), 43, 66, 125
International anticommunist Brigade, 25
Iredell, James, 86
ITT (International Telephone and Telegraph), 73

J

Jackson, Brooks, 105
Jackson, Robert, 85, 151
Jaworski, Leon, 19, 118
John F. Kennedy Library and Museum, 116
Johnson, Lyndon B., 15, *26*, 80, 123, 160
Jones, Elaine, 116
Jordan, Barbara, 71–76, *74*

K

Kalmbach, Herbert W., 5, 37, 164
Kelley, Jack, 104
Kelly, Harry, 151
Kennedy, Edward, 31, 35, 116, 125
Kennedy, John F., 4, *26*, 31, 73, 80, 92, 116, 123
King, Martin Luther Jr., 79–80
Kissinger, Henry, 5, 15, 100
Kleindienst, Richard, 5, 45, 163
Koenig, Louis W., 13–20, 94–95
Koran, 102–103

Kraft, Joseph, 151–152

L

Lay, Kenneth, 120
Leper, Paul, 27
Lewis, Alfred E., 21–29
Lewis, John, 116
Liddy, G. Gordon
    autobiography, 65
    Dean and, 155–157
    FBI and, 6
    Hunt and, 154
    Mitchell and, 65
    photograph, *156*
    Playboy interview, 153–161
    Plumbers unit and, 15
    trial and conviction, 18, 144, 151
    Watergate break-in and, 6, 16, 18, 65, 123–124
Lincoln, Abraham, 131–132
Livingston, Edward, 86
Locke, John, 94–95
Loory, Stuart, 32
Los Angeles Times, 32, 151
Lukas, J. Anthony, 30–38

M

MacKinnon, George, 93
Madison, James, 73, 75
Magruder, Jeb Stuart, 6, 16, 36, 143, 164–165
Marsh, John, 112
Marshall, John, 86
Martinez, Eugenio R., 23–24
McCarthy, Joseph, 85
McCarthyism, 85
McClellan, Scott, 103